13.67

THE BEGINNING OF WISDOM

THE BEGINNING OF WISDOM

The 1946–47 Otts Lectures
at Davidson College, North Carolina

by

EMILE CAILLIET

Stuart Professor of Christian Philosophy
Princeton Theological Seminary

NEW YORK

Fleming H. Revell Company

LONDON AND GLASGOW

NEW YORK 10: 158 Fifth Avenue
LONDON, E.C. 4: 29 Ludgate Hill
GLASGOW, C. 2: 229 Bothwell Street

To

JOHN ALEXANDER MACKAY

in a common commitment

A MESSAGE TO THE READER

For the last twenty years the author has lived on the American campus, that is, in quarters where no issue can be dodged by those who would be granted a hearing.

Any student worthy of the name knows that he has to be intellectually honest. In the manner of Malebranche, he goes on repeating, "My ideas resist me," that is, "I think as I do because I cannot think otherwise and keep my self-respect." In this connection it would appear that most of those who drift toward agnosticism do so against their own wish. To expose them and their present status through harsh words will no longer do. In fact, they would be only too happy to find a working solution to their religious problem within the Christian fold. Many of them are willing to admit that their quest for wisdom has led them to an impasse.

In their anxiety to be intellectually respectable college students and well educated people in general have sought after such forms of wisdom as shirk the "foolishness" implied in Christianity. However pleasant such "by-path meadows" may be, they must lead to confusion and finally to despair if, as the author has come to believe, the basic message of the Bible is true.

This little book is patterned along the lines of the quest for true wisdom. Instead of dealing with generalities or abstractions, the author starts from the specific human situation of the cultured man of good-will. With words which avoid technicalities and philosophical jargon, he attempts to accompany the seeker through objections and problems until a right Biblical perspective is restored and the case for commitment is stated with singleness of purpose. Only those works immediately accessible to the layman for reference are mentioned.

Thus it is the author's fervent hope that the following pages will be of some help to the rank and file reader as well as to the "intelligentsia," often unfairly stigmatized by candid souls.

E. C.

Princeton, N. J.

Christianity cannot allow itself to be reduced to nature or to any process in nature, if for no other reason than that it purports to be the revelation of the *nature* of nature. It sees nature through a certain window that was once opened in history—a specific event or span of events in history. Looking through this window, it tells us what nature is, namely, the creation of God and the manifestation of his continuing creativity. Seen through the window of the Christian revelation in history, nature takes on a new dimension. It becomes a different nature from that with which the scientist (quite legitimately for his purpose) deals. The fallacy involved in the use of the label "naturalism," is that of reductionism. It is the fallacy of explaining the higher by reducing it to the lower, and such an explanation always casts away the essential qualitative character of the higher. . . .

Christianity comes to us with no less a claim than that its affirmations of the nature of the cosmos in which man lives are the last word in the unveiling of reality. Compared with its affirmations, all other affirmations of the nature of reality represent a partial, truncated and, when put forward as ultimate, a distorted and debased form of truth. Such affirmations are the actual myths to which modern man has been clinging on his unsteady descent to nihilism. It is high time that the Christian faith disengage itself from these modern myths and set out boldly to win a culture gone pagan to the truth as it has been unveiled in Jesus Christ.

CHARLES CLAYTON MORRISON.

CONTENTS

V. TOWARD A BIBLICAL PERSPECTIVE

VI. THE PATH ACROSS THIS WILDERNESS

VII. "DOING THE TRUTH"

CHAPTER I

Groping for Light

THIS CHRISTIAN CIVILIZATION

THE CIVILIZATION of our Western world is Christian by birth and by right.

At the dawn of the nineteenth century a great French writer Chateaubriand could rightly state in *Le Génie du Christianisme* that the Christian religion is "the most poetic, the most humane, and the most favorable to liberty, to the arts and to letters"; that the modern world owes it "everything, from agriculture to the abstract sciences, from hospitals for the poor to temples wrought by Michelangelo and decorated by Raphael."[1]

Observe great Christians at work, and consider the abundant blessing derived from such men as John Wesley, William Wilberforce, Lord Shaftsbury, William Gladstone, Abraham Lincoln, David Livingstone, François Coillard, Louis Pasteur, William Booth, Albert Schweitzer, William Carey, to name only a few. Trace the influence of Christianity, say, on the status of

[1] Chateaubriand, *Œuvres Complètes,* Paris: Ladvocat, 1826, v. 11, *Génie du Christianisme I,* 21.

woman, on child life, on the outlawing of slavery, in all beneficent work among the poor, the sick, and the captive, in the world of economics at large, in the advent of constitutional government, in the fight against illiteracy, and in the foundation of schools and universities. What a liberation on every hand, in every realm of endeavor!

What actually happened is that Christianity gave to natural man a new vision of the universe, and of his own being. In his message and in his works, nay in his vicarious suffering on the Cross, Jesus Christ revealed the supreme value of the human soul in the sight of God. Such parables as those of the lost sheep, the lost coin, and the lost son emphasized the precious character of the individual. Jesus brought to His own followers the fatherhood of God, with a new sense of brotherhood among themselves. From their salvation the disciples derived real freedom, according to the oft-quoted verse, "Ye shall know the truth and the truth shall make you free." This is the message that spread the cause of liberalism among multitudes.

With the revelation of the greatness of the human soul there came into man's life a new sense of disquietude—man being described in the words of Péguy as "a monster of uneasiness." Paganism denied anguish and reached to perfection. The serenity of its art could no longer satisfy the soul of man, however perfect this art may have been in form. Should the reader answer this assertion by calling to mind the depth of Sophocles and the sacred horror of *Œdipus King* in the face of an obscure destiny, then allow me in turn to point to the inner conflicts of Hamlet or of Lady Macbeth! What new depths have not been fathomed with Shakespeare! Likewise, picture side by side the Athena Parthenos of Phidias dedicated to the goddess Minerva, and one of our sublime cathedrals whose restless, unfinished lines rise up to heaven in tormented search for the living God! As do, in fact, the *Summa Theologica* of Thomas Aquinas and the *Commedia* of Dante. And since we are speaking of Dante, compare his treatment of love with that of Horace. Christian love learned its language from the mystics' communion with Christ. The search for the Grail set the pattern for the knight's search for his lady love. Thus faith soon inspired chivalry and moral nobility. A new sense of mystery pervades the paintings of da Vinci and of Rembrandt; the same uneasiness of which I have just spoken is felt in the sculpture of our churches, in the sonatas of Beethoven, and in the longings of Bach and Cesar Franck that seem to echo a prayer of Saint Theresa. So in the whole Christian body there arose a sense of warm fellowship before the call of the Divine, an irresistible urge toward a higher plane where Love would have the last word. Pascal, after he had experimented on the vacuum in the physical realm, was to experience the vacuum in the spiritual realm and to write his immortal pages on the misery of man without God.

Everyone will admit in his heart and mind that this world of men and affairs is the better for having been the abode of Christ in His earthly life. A moral transformation has taken place wherein notions of human equality, of human dignity, or simply of humanity, have become matters of course; and yet these were unknown to the ancients. Human thought has risen to heights heretofore undreamt of in the realm of speculation. Reason has been enabled to work out its demonstrations from our knowledge of things material with far more assurance, since revelation has enlightened its path by releasing the glow of its divine goal. For many a Christian thinker intelligence has taken on its true meaning, namely, "the faculty to read."

The supernatural has become a part of our horizon. It is no longer a stranger in nature; it is above the nature that our limited faculties are able to perceive. Furthermore, Christians know it to be more real than the reality of mere sense experience. In vain will naturalists advise them to discard the crown and return to Protagoras, and to his contention that man is the measure of all things. As they persist in their attitude, monstrous forms of "substitute" religion arise to make them rudely aware of their error. We cannot go back. It will be Jesus Christ or an Adolph Hitler; Christianity or some man-made myth of racism.

So, while it is true that civilization had developed

before Christ, just as new forms of culture have since arisen apart from Christ, we may nevertheless affirm that the best in our Western culture is Christian by birth and by right. It is still more true that civilization at large, as we have come to speak of it, has been wonderfully transformed, and in a unique way has been made fruitful, by the leaven of Christianity.

GHOSTS ON THE CAMPUS

Our Western civilization is Christian by birth and by right. The same is true of our liberal arts tradition. A striking symbol of this fact is that practically every college used to be built around a chapel. It is for this very reason, for example, that Oxford has deserved the name of "the city of spires." The history of all great continental universities has been repeated at Harvard, Yale, William and Mary. Of the first one hundred and nineteen colleges founded east of the Mississippi River, one hundred and four were Christian and all of them were primarily Christian in purpose.

Yet the spiritual vitality and influence which came to American education through Christianity has reached a low point today. Only an intensive revival can save our Christian liberal arts tradition from disintegration and futility, from what Rosalind Murray has called *the good pagan's failure*.

To many a student, for example, the Bible has become only a monument of English prose. The distinguished poet T. S. Eliot says in this connection that he could easily fulminate for a whole hour against the men of letters who have gone into ecstasies over "the Bible as literature," the Bible as "the noblest monument of English prose." To him, those who talk of the Bible as "a monument of English prose" are merely admiring it as "a monument over the grave of Christianity." The Bible, he explains, has had "a literary influence upon English literature *not* because it has been considered as literature, but because it has been considered as the report of the Word of God. And the fact that men of letters now discuss it as literature probably indicates the *end* of its 'literary influence.'" [2]

The religious problem is the ultimate issue in the life of the student. A satisfactory answer to it would give meaning to the whole process of integration implied in his education. Yet the Christian faith remains the objectionable item on the campus, unless it is mentioned as a remnant of a pre-scientific age and as such becomes the pretext for some wise rationalistic assertions. The late President Dwight of Yale University once remarked, "It has always been my experience that those teachers who are religious never mention it in the classroom, whereas those who are antagonistic to religion are always talking about it to the students." [3]

[2] Quoted by John A. Mackay in *Theology Today,* v. I, nr. 3, Oct. 1944, 288-289.
[3] William Lyon Phelps, *Autobiography With Letters,* Oxford University Press, 1939, p. 297.

As a rule, no positive conclusion is ever reached in the course of such discussions that would be likely to lead the student to a committed life. As David F. Swenson put it, the "professor" in the Kierkegaardian sense "cannot inherit, since he excludes himself from the realm of spirit by evading the claims of inwardness, passion, and decisive action." [4] Intellectual speculation becomes a substitute for a walk of consecration. How searching is the statement of the Letter to Timothy concerning persons that are "ever learning and never able to come to the knowledge of the truth." We have a name for such intellectuals: we call them *dilettanti*. For them speculation has become an end in itself. They *lend* themselves to all sorts of attitudes without surrendering to any cause whatsoever. We should not insist on this infirm state of mind were it not so prevalent, though not always developed to the extreme. We are merely reminded of that Aristotelian gourmand of the *Ethica Nicomachea* who "prayed that his throat might become longer than a crane's, implying that it was the contact he took pleasure in." [5]

The objective approach to education, in stressing both the possibilities and the limitations of our human faculties, has done much to encourage that skepticism which we may describe as playful. In fact, the Greek

---

[4] David F. Swenson, *Something about Kierkegaard,* Minneapolis: Augsburg Publishing House, 1941, p. 93.

[5] *Ethica Nicomachea,* translated by W. D. Ross, Oxford University Press, 1925, Book III, 10, 1118a.

word *skepsis* means *research,* and research, like hunting and fishing, tends to become a pleasant occupation—with the difference that the hunter and the fisherman are as a rule interested in the result of their sport. Yet we know, do we not?—that they would disregard the game or the catch were it simply offered them for the asking.

Such playfulness, combined in varying degrees with a false objectivity, attended by a natural instinct for a sheltered life and the usual anxiety to be intellectually respectable, makes up for a certain type of "academic" attitude which is, alas, widespread. Professor Theodore M. Green of Princeton and Yale Universities seems to have happily defined this detached and essentially cowardly attitude when he branded it "one of endless investigation and argument without decision or commitment—of never taking sides on anything, of never committing oneself to anything." If I sense accurately the feelings of our returned veterans they have but little patience with this variety of tight-rope acrobatics, which the mere academicians of yesteryear seemed to consider a prerequisite for the granting of degrees.

To my mind, Irvin Edman in *Philosopher's Holiday* has presented in an isolated chapter entitled "An Irishman among the Brahmins," a perfect preview of the scenes of holy impatience which sometimes must unfold among our veterans. George O'Connor has gone to his professor, who tells the story, to ask whether a course of his in the philosophy of religion was "worth taking," or whether it was "just another course." Let us now listen to the amplification rendered by our eager young student: Does this course, he asks, "really give you new ideas, or do something to your old ones? Does it make you over, or give you a new world?" [6] Having finally tried the course—and a seminar besides—having tried even to enter into the necessary discipline of this type of intellectual life, young George one day decides to leave the college, with this remark intensely expressed: "I can't stand it any more, I don't see how you can. . . . The place is too confoundedly intellectual. All the intellectual words, but no ideas with life in them. Ghosts of the mind walking around the campus." [7] Of course, his professor sees him to be wrong, and tries to make a case for his own philosophy of education. As I read the story, however, I could not avoid thinking that even this distinguished scholar had not fully understood what the student was driving at.

What this student was driving at is as simple as it is natural. He was tired of "debunking" great things and great men, and no longer appreciated his education in accordance with the enjoyment he derived from

[6] Irvin Edman, *Philosopher's Holiday*, The Viking Press, 1938, reproduced in Penguin Books, 1943, p. 49.

[7] *Ibid.*, p. 50.

it. He was not against this or that philosophy, as much as against the sophisticated use of philosophy. He no longer found pleasure in reviving doubts before they had had a chance to disappear. This neverending inquiry got the better of him, and he began to regard as mere distraction the dealing in clear ideas which really were small ideas. For, above all, students want to know whether there is "a meaning to it all," whether or not it is "a tale told by an idiot." They do not understand the reason for this prevalent self-imposed taboo of transcendence. They want to know whether or not, in the words of James Thomson in his *City of Dreadful Night*

> ". . . none can pierce the vast black veil uncertain
> Because there is no light beyond the curtain;
> . . . all is vanity and nothingness." [8]

The students want to know whether or not the Christian faith matters, and if it matters how much it *does* matter. They want freedom for self-deception. They refuse to distinguish between what is practicable and what is true. They demand an answer.

THE AFTERMATH OF SURRENDER

We may safely lay down the principle that the average student is eager to find out all he can about

---

[8] James Thomson, *The City of Dreadful Night and other Poems*, London: Reeves and Turner, 1880, xxi, p. 55.

Christianity and ready to rise up to the occasion. He does not see why it should take more "nerve" to be a Communist than a Christian. He is in dead earnest about it. Like Kierkegaard at the age of twenty-two, he wants clarity with respect to what he ought to do. He wants to find the Idea for which he can live and die. With the author of *Concluding Unscientific Postscript,* he realizes that "existence constitutes the highest interest of the existing individual," and that "his interest in his existence constitutes his reality." [9] Yet there is no Christian answer available amidst the confusion of contemporary thought on religion. As every program by now has become a compromise, the religious program on the campus is merely concerned with giving students a sense of social responsibility in community living and with promoting, as a complement to the last, what the Harvard report calls "the completely good life." So it would seem to be, for such confusion has muffled the voice of the Church. As a consequence, educational institutions have been left in the dark about this basic issue, and disintegration of our culture as a whole would appear to have resulted.

As the only true integrating Principle is lacking, on every side we find emphasized the analytical approach. The specialists have entered the scene, every

[9] Søren Kierkegaard, *Concluding Unscientific Postscript to the Philosophical Fragments,* 1846, trans. by David F. Swenson and Walter Lowrie, Princeton University Press, p. 279.

intellectual discipline pulling away from the center. Sometimes various interests have managed to unite on the campus in order to secure a share of the spoils, whether in the form of larger credits for the purchase of books, a more active part in important committees, a wider area in course offerings, or perhaps heightened prestige in student opinion. Thus partial integrations, most of them shallow or one-sided, have come about on the very boundary of the curriculum.

In vain, committees have been appointed to try to make a coherent speech out of this confusion of tongues. The main trouble is that the center was hardly ever heard from; and, unfortunately, when it was heard from, the voice was incoherent enough to be ignored.

Practically every college, as we pointed out above, had been built around a chapel and, so to speak, had learned its language in the sanctuary. Yet—at least in our Reformed tradition—the vision was lost. In some cases the Church became so afraid of the College that the two eventually were no longer on speaking terms. The Church had transformed itself into an impregnable fortress. The bridges across the moat were drawn up, and to this day invective is heard from both sides of the moat. Name-calling seems to be in order between the "obscurantist orthodox" and the "skeptical professor."

In other cases the churchman began to realize the extent of his supposed ignorance, and so it came about that he applied for readmission to the College so as to learn the vernacular which is spoken there. He even spoke it with a pebble in his mouth. Thus were permanent bridges thrown across the moat which surrounded the mighty fortress once provisioned for eternity. As Kierkegaard put it, the fortress was transformed into a country-seat.[10]

Let us view the result of such collaboration. The so-called "mythology" of the book of *Revelation* is being rejected as "grotesque and even immoral," and the book discarded because the pictures in it are considered bad, whatever the merits of the affirmations they illustrate. The message of the Kingdom has yielded to those of Bacon's *New Atlantis,* Campanella's *City of the Sun,* and to the idealizations of William Morris and H. G. Wells. Our persevering churchman even tackles Sir Thomas More's *Utopia,* although he will admit that to him it is one of the most boring things to read and that, confidentially, it suggests one of the most disappointing places in which to live.

It would be a mistake, however, to suppose that the life of the churchman in the midst of college students is one of perfect understanding and peace. In his *Autobiography,* the late Professor William Lyon

[10] Walter Lowrie, *A Short Life of Kierkegaard,* Princeton University Press, 1942, p. 234.

Phelps of Yale University tells how the divinity students at Yale were often shocked by the alcoholic enthusiasm of sophomores returning from Boston late at night. But, he adds, "the shock was nothing to that received by the sophomores when they asked the candidates for the Christian ministry about their religious beliefs. At the end of the year the sophomores, on being asked if they wanted to continue occupying rooms in the same building with the divinity men, answered, "No! we don't want to room with those . . . atheists!" [11] An interesting story, that. Certainly we should take it with at least two grains of salt, one for Professor Phelps, who must have written it with his tongue in his cheek, and the other for the sophomores, whose sensitivity in matters of orthodox belief seems to have been greatly exaggerated, especially in view of their evident lack of repentance in the matter of drinking. The divinity men did not drink. They found a nobler form of recreation in "bull sessions" about fine points of theology. During such sessions the wildest opinions must have been openly expressed, to the scandal, no doubt, of some homely sophomore who had not taken the Boston train.

What is interesting is that in this entire argument we have some elementary truth on either side. While keeping in mind that we are dealing here with a caricature calling for a sense of humor in its interpreta-

[11] *Autobiography with Letters, op. cit.,* p. 272.

tion, we must admit that a caricature is always revealing. It brings out essential features from among the
least flattering. It is, in a way, a mild indictment pro-
nounced with an amused smile, one which does not
leave any scar. Yet a sensitive soul will find in it
opportunity for self-examination. The sophomores saw
the divinity men's censure as sheer blue-law moraliz-
ing, unsupported by deep religious convictions, but
simply standing for a self-sufficient code of observances. Such puritanical codes may formulate certain
rules that pertain to the Decalogue. Even in such
cases, not only the motives that inspire them, but the
ways in which they are often enforced, are likely to
remind one more of *The Scarlet Letter* than of the
letter of the Bible, let alone its spirit. Is it unrighteous
to play cards, to go to the movies, or to dance? I hear
One suggest with a gentle smile, "We have piped for
you, and you would not dance." I am reminded further that this same gracious One was ostracized by
self-righteous people as a "wine-bibber" and a "glutton"
because he was seen in the company of tax-gatherers
and sinners. In the words of Basil King in his *Conquest
of Fear*:

"Our notion of morals hardly ever rises above the average
custom of the community in which we happen to live. . . .
The consequence is that our cities, villages, countrysides,
and social groupings are filled with men and women moral

enough as far as the custom of the country goes, but quite noticeably unrighteous.

"It is also a fact that where you find one or two virtues singled out for observance and the rest obscured, there you find, too, throngs of outwardly 'moral' people with corroded hearts. Villages, churches, and all the quieter communities are notorious for this, the peculiarity having formed for a hundred and fifty years the stock-in-trade of novelists. Sobriety and continence being more or less in evidence, the assumption is that all the requirements have been fulfilled. The community is 'moral' notwithstanding the back-bitings, heart-burnings, slanders, cheatings, envies, hatreds, and bitternesses that may permeate it through and through. As I write, the cramped, venomous, unlovely life of the American small town is the favorite theme of our authors and readers of fiction." [12]

Now that divinity men and sophomores have met on the campus, we may begin to discover what is basically wrong with our notions of Christianity and with those of our Liberal Arts education.

Christianity seems to be merely concerned with being good and doing good. It has been flattened out to the point of being identified with the Aristotelian doctrine of the mean. Anyone who is at all interested in finding out what such a surrender amounts to may read side by side the Sermon on the Mount and the Fourth Book of the *Ethica Nicomachea,* and may com-

[12] Basil King. *The Conquest of Fear,* Doubleday, 1921, republished in The New Home Library Edition, 1942, pp. 126, 127.

pare the Christian denying of self with the Aristotelian teaching of the ways of being truly proud and of despising "justly," as the ancient philosopher put it.

A vague religiosity deprived of intellectual backbone has become nothing more than "dope." The beautiful word "liberal" has been made to apply to caricatures. With Dean Swift, we would know what a "liberal" carpenter would be; he might have a board too long at one end. A "liberal" physician might give you a little more medicine. A "liberal" chemist might not tell you the truth of the analysis. A "liberal" astronomer might count too many stars. A "liberal" philosopher might say too much about the science of truth. A "liberal" farmer might sow the seed too thick. A "liberal" milkman might give the pump handle one more stroke downward. . . . What then does a "liberal" preacher mean? There is serious confusion of thought as to what Christianity really implies, and the religious problem in our higher education is merely an aspect of the general confusion. Or is it that we should practice Christianity without believing in it?

On every side we are faced with a failure to come to grips with the central affirmations of the Christian faith. Mysteries degenerate into problems. It was suggested in a recent thesis submitted in partial fulfilment of the degree of Doctor of Philosophy at Columbia University in the faculty of political science, that our churches,[13] having shown some uncertainty as to their function, should bend their efforts toward social amelioration.

Having turned into something that may be studied as a problem, religion has now become a subject for scientific investigation, while the Bible is looked on as providing material for secular anthropological research. Meanwhile, our educational set-up is without intellectual, moral, and spiritual leadership, and our civilization misses the mark to go finally into bankruptcy. In the words of a Belgian scholar, every victory of modern man "has turned into defeat. Colonization was followed by slavery, industrialism by the exploitation of the workers or unemployment, science by the last refinement in the art of warfare. Every weapon which man forged for himself and which was supposed to subject the blind forces of nature to his will was twisted in his hands and turned against himself." [14]

Let us not say that we planned it that way! Only a man like William the Conqueror would interpret a great fall as an omen of victory. Freeman tells us in his *History of the Norman Conquest* how William's foot slipped as he became the first armed man to land on English soil, so that he fell with both hands on the

[13] Joseph Van Vleck, Jr., *Our Changing Churches,* A Study in Church Leadership, New York: Association Press, 1937.

[14] Emile Cammaerts, *The Flower of Grass,* New York: Harper and Brothers, 1945, p. 86.

ground. As a loud cry was uttered at the evil omen, the ready wit of William failed him not. "By the splendor of God," he exclaimed, "I have taken seizure of my kingdom; the earth of England is in my hand." But this is not an appropriate time for ready wit on our part, neither is it the earth of England which we have in our hands.

To sum up this painful indictment, then, let us admit that organized Christianity has now become a confusion of tongues. As such it is unable for the present to inspire and direct the religious reorientation of our higher education. In matters of conduct other groups have the ascendance over our churches. Sociologists and political scientists now make a point of studying these same churches in the light of a glorified dread of innovation whereby the prime obligation of the faithful is conformity to the pattern set by the group. Schiller's admonition to a young poet, as we find it in his *Ninth Esthetic Letter,* becomes pertinent in such a situation, "Live with your time, but be not the creature of your time. Give your contemporaries, not that which they are disposed to praise, but that which they need."

I have called this a "painful indictment," and so it is, on my part. I am well aware that criticism is hardly, if ever, constructive. Do not criticize me. Do not criticize them. Love me and help me; love them and help them. Like Herodotus in his *History,* I do not

dispute whether ancient tales be true, but merely begin
with these wrongs whereof I myself have knowledge.
In the manner of Socrates, at the beginning of Plato's
Apology,[15] all I ask is that you give heed to the truth
of my words.

THE CHRISTIAN MINISTRY VINDICATED

Yet, in all fairness, it must now be admitted that
the Christian ministry is being shamefully abused
nowadays. I know our ministers. On many occasions
I have spent days with them and shared their concern.
I have seen them at grips with tremendous problems.
I have seen them buying books they could hardly
afford and take these back to a distant parish, only to
find their reading and meditation constantly disturbed
by all sorts of requests. The minister need never be told
that "to minister" means "to serve." He is constantly
reminded of this, as he smilingly submits to the most
unheard-of chores. Yet he feels that he must keep
his culture up-to-date. The most disturbing books call
for his attention. Do they leave him a gospel to proclaim?

For instance: A recent historical and comparative
study of the "Idea" of Salvation in the world's great

---

[15] "Never mind the manner, which may or may not be good; but
think only of the truth of my words, and give heed to that: let the
speaker speak truly and the judge decide justly." (Plato's *Apology* of
Socrates, translated from the Greek by Benjamin Jowett, Portland, Maine:
Thomas B. Mosher, 1910, p. 5.)

living religions reveals so many *other* paths in what is called *Man's Quest for Salvation*.[16] Meanwhile, the minister's Bible seems to shrink every day. The Old Testament is said no longer to make sense as a whole, and many a thoughtful scholar is uneasy about it. A new Marcionism pervades the Church as the New Testament is claimed to be the only pertinent revelation of a God of Love. But then the amount of accepted historical data in this same New Testament would appear to grow less. At least, it would seem so if, for instance, we are to proceed from the presuppositions of certain scholars who like to call themselves "objective." For some time and until recently, the approach to the Gospels has been guarded by Form-Criticism, to which, let us admit, we owe a great deal of gratitude for useful technical service rendered, as we do in fact to "Liberalism" in general.

Form-Criticism was led to stress the dependence of the Gospel tradition on the early Christian community which handed it down. It stressed it to such an extent, in fact, that it tended to historical agnosticism in matters of faith. While such scholars as Martin Dibelius were satisfied with giving credit to the community for having wisely preserved vital parts of the Gospel, zealous Form-critics went much further. They claimed that the community actually *produced*

[16] Charles S. Braden, *Man's Quest for Salvation*, an historical and comparative study of the idea of Salvation in the world's great living religions, Chicago, New York: Willett, Clark and Co., 1941.

most of the said tradition. Once more, the initiative was seen to be passing from God to man, as often has been the case in past interpretations of Christianity. Naturalistic tendencies we have always with us.

In this instance, consequences for the interpretation of "Old Stories" such as the Passion narratives were far-reaching. In many a resulting treatment of the subject the interest is seen to shift from the Resurrection to the "Resurrection-faith." This faith is then seen to be centering around the One who surely must have been the Messiah, however reticent He may have been on the subject. Such reticence as surrounded the "Messianic secret" then becomes the measure of all Messianic sayings, nay, of all authoritative sayings by our Lord. Such is the type of reasoning which indeed makes accepted historical data grow less—at least for a while. The fact is, it strikes at the very roots of the Gospel or "Goods News." But, then, many intellectuals in our day would argue that this same "Good News" is no longer essential to "religion" as they have come to think of it.

The most lasting impression that secular scholars would seem to have received from their contact with Bible categories is that the Semite knows of no shade of thought. They prefer the company of the Greek to whom γνῶσις results from intellectual progress alone, once the stage of what Lévy-Bruhl called a "prelogical" or "mystical" way of thinking is well-nigh over-passed, and the level of ἐπιστήμη, science, has been reached. According to Lévy-Bruhl in fact, the "pre-logical" or "mystical" stage is never completely over-passed, even in the most "enlightened" communities.[17] This may explain why mysticism in our day invades even the domain of science, in spite of the fact that nature's gods do not prove to be more convincing than *maya,* or illusion, the Oriental dismissal of the world.

Although the present lecture must proceed further in the inquiry at hand, we already see why it will not be enough for subsequent lectures to come to grips with positivism or naturalism. There looms in our midst a far more subtle challenge to Christianity than that of positivism or naturalism, namely, the challenge of vague forms of mysticism. While always anxious to safeguard the genuine Christian experience of direct communion with the living God of the Bible, we constantly beware of contemporary forms of pan-psychism, which are basically heathen in character.

Higher forms of Greek mysticism we have always with us, to be sure. Identifying ultimate truth with beauty, a cosmic optimism tends to find in goodness the supreme reason of all that exists. This is a faith also, a noble faith likely to tempt those who have progressively abandoned a specifically Biblical creed because they thought they could not otherwise. The

[17] Cf. Lévy-Bruhl's own clarification of the subject in the Herbert Spencer Lecture he delivered at Oxford on May 29, 1931, Oxford: at the Clarendon Press, 1931, especially pp. 21, 26, 27.

time always comes when Christianity is seen to have been as much of a support for Greek mysticism as Greek mysticism is usually credited to have been for Christianity. In this connection such apologists as Justin Martyr have probably achieved more lasting results for Hellenistic yearnings than for the Jewish hope.

Such yearnings on the part of great minds are likely to find their ultimate in the acknowledgment of the limitations of human nature. We must admit in this connection that there are negations which prove to be more deeply religious than many an "orthodox" affirmation. A history of "negative" theology since the days of Anselm of Canterbury would illustrate this fact. We would further agree that God's purpose makes light of man's pretense; that there is no situation which He cannot redeem; that His sovereignty will make of any theologian the most unprofitable, if not the most ridiculous, servant. All that, we know; and because we know it, Christian charity would have us go to extremes in our efforts at understanding the religious quest of our fellow men.

Yet we also know that the *essentia* of Bible-Christianity is that God, who in many and various ways spoke of old by the Prophets, has in the fulness of time spoken to us by a Son whom He appointed heir of all things. We know that disciples were commissioned by this same Son to go and *proclaim* the Gospel, and that He promised He would be with them always, to the close of the age. Such considerations are so essential in fact that, with due respect for the conclusions of a reverent Bible scholarship, I, for one, find myself unable to believe that our Living God could have at all been indifferent to the final formulation and presentation of His Word. The fact is, the Bible is most specific on this matter of inspiration.

Such is forever the vindication of the Christian ministry in the face of natural religion and of human speculation. By the same token there will always be a tension between the privilege of free inquiry on the part of the college man, and the necessity of proclaiming the Gospel message on the part of the churchman. As the minister gets a new awareness of his tremendous responsibility in this, our scientific age, he will also come to realize that he has a great deal to be thankful for.

The "Liberals" who, as we have just seen, raised intricate problems in his path, would seem to be fighting a defensive battle at the present time. Not only has "the peril of modernizing Jesus" been admitted,[18] but the whole "Liberal" interpretation of the Bible, which was taking shape along the lines of categories foreign to the Book, no longer seems to fit the facts. And lo and behold, the materials resulting from dec-

[18] Cf. H. J. Cadbury, *The Peril of Modernizing Jesus,* New York: Macmillan, 1927.

ades of analysis slowly fall piece by piece into their proper places, until a rich pattern of Bible unity is discerned—more imposing than of old. Once more, human fears would prove to have been in vain, as was the case when the universe of Newton replaced the Aristotelian conception in the mind of a new age.

THE NEED FOR REORIENTATION

Yet there would be disagreement even on this point. There are eyes which do not see; minds which become absorbed in one particular detail, or isolate a certain line of analysis; methods which dispute the same ground while taking of it different, if not opposite, views. Again, the worth of such views is often judged according to chronology, the latest book being generally supposed to be the best. I once witnessed a man's faith being shaken up by the reading of a single book, and I still believe that there had been in that case too drastic an interpretation of Emerson's "Essay on Self-Reliance." You may remember the passage: "With consistency a great soul has simply nothing to do." For the Christian faith was involved, and the man in question was familiar with the Gospel-before-the-Gospels. In view of his knowledge, he should have been aware of the presence in the primitive tradition of this early nucleus, that is, Jesus' word— "Blessed is he who shall find no stumbling block in me."

Professor Reinhold Niebuhr concludes a recent

"Hazen Pamphlet," entitled *The Contribution of Religion to Cultural Unity,* with the statement that the resources for a program of religious reorientation of our higher education "must come out of the religious community and our religious institutions." He lays down the principle that "the primary responsibility for resolving the contradiction between religious obscurantism and religious defeatism rests upon them and not upon the educational institutions." This is an interesting remark. What strikes us is the fact that college people seem to disagree with Professor Niebuhr in that *they* take up this matter of formulating a religious policy for the benefit of our higher education. For example, Professor Goodenough writes his book *Religious Tradition and Myth* as one who realizes that "the loneliness and inarticulateness of the modern intellectual's religious life is robbing our civilization of one of its deepest needs, the spiritual contribution we can give it." [19]

Toward the end of his book he submits as an example of such "loneliness" and "inarticulateness" the case of one of the most distinguished of American scholars, a man who never goes to church because he feels, rightly or wrongly, that modern Christianity has nothing to offer him. We would suggest at this point a fact that college men are wont to overlook,

[19] Erwin R. Goodenough, *Religious Tradition and Myth,* New Haven: Yale University Press, 1937, p. 11.

namely, the fact that the Church often provides the average man with the only type of higher education to which he has access. It is only in church that the great issues of life are opened up to him, however imperfectly. But, to proceed, this same American scholar stated to Professor Goodenough in private conversation: "I am a believer. I believe in the Power-not-ourselves, and with that Power I am in daily relations." [20]

This pragmatic and agnostic definition of God as "The Power-not-ourselves" is a mere abbreviation of that of Matthew Arnold in his book, *Literature and Dogma.* According to the author of *Religious Tradition and Myth,* it is the definition underlying the creed of many an intellectual in our day, whether he knows and admits it or not. It is Professor Goodenough's own definition. Like Matthew Arnold, he found it in the earliest traditions of Judaism. The similarity to Matthew Arnold appears again in their common quotation from Micah: "He hath showed thee, O man, what is good: and what doth the Lord require of thee, but to do justly, and to love mercy, and to walk humbly with thy God?" There even comes to light, as in *Literature and Dogma,* a certain amount of confusion between sheer morality and genuine righteousness. Yet a definite progress may be noted in the fact that, unlike Matthew Arnold, Professor Goodenough

[20] *Ibid.,* p. 91.

remains on speaking terms with "The Power-not-ourselves."

For the last one hundred years some of the most highly cultured men concerned with religion in colleges and universities, in this country and abroad, have submitted religion to the harshest criticism. They have struck the rock roughly at the point where God appears as the Power-not-ourselves, who, somehow, makes for righteousness and sends the blessed one back to his fellow men "with a richness not of the common earth." [21] It would be hard to overestimate the significance of such a fact.

Agnosticism having been given full sway, we are allowed to uncover, as it were, the rock-bed on which a sane Bible-Christianity might be rebuilt, and there precisely because Bible-Christianity had been built on it originally. But, pray, does Micah's great pronouncement refer to morals only? Decidedly not. Morals have chiefly to do with the observance of a social code. They do not necessarily imply the "cleaning of the cup." Righteousness has to do rather with a new God-given direction to life. In the words of J. S. Whale:

"For the Old Testament, as for the New, righteousness does not mean the righteousness of moral perfection, the excellence of a man whose moral class is 'alpha plus.' It means being right with God, that is, being put right or acquitted at His throne of grace. Righteousness is God's

[21] *Ibid.*, p. 97.

demand because it is God's gift. All Israel's characteristic institutions operate within this context or covenant of grace." [22]

Such basic notions bring us as far from vague mysticism as they do from a mere code of morality, which also is very important, as we hope to show later. Micah's great pronouncement refers to the basic element of personal religion, on the campus as elsewhere, in terms of *walk*. Thus the Introduction to the Shorter Moffat Bible, published by Harper's, gives the gist of the Book in these terms: "It is pre-eminently the record of God's disclosure of Himself and His high purposes in creating mankind, and the spiritual resources available for those who seek to do His will." Thus our quest brings us face to face with the supreme issue.

THE ISSUE

Is the Bible the record of the Living God's Self-disclosure, or is it merely a saga of wishful thinking on the part of man? Is the language of the Bible merely "thrown out" in the empty space at some imaginary object of consciousness? Does its eloquence and poetry go to some Beyond, great or small, or does it bounce back with the splendid resonance of great poetic utterances, only to leave us with a sense of frustration as we wonder how seriously it should be taken?

[22] J. S. Whale, *Christian Doctrine*, New York: Macmillan, 1941, p. 78.

Dr. Fosdick has given full acknowledgment to this problem at the beginning of his *Guide to Understanding the Bible*. What he likes to call "the unfolding of ideas" recorded in Scripture would, he admits, "represent not so much discovery as illusion, were there not a spiritual world to be discovered. Any one, therefore, holding a religious rather than a materialistic philosophy will think of the process of Biblical development as dual—seen from one side, a human achievement; seen from the other, a divine self-revelation." [23]

In other words, all human beings dispute the same ground with the same make-up. Together, they confront the same reality—nay, the same Bible, the same Christ. Yet they view this same reality from two different angles. Some have a man-centered, naturalistic, outlook; others have a God-centered, a Christian, outlook.

"We must wager," as Pascal put it. In a domain beyond our reach there is a "game" going on, the meaning of which differs according to whether God is real or not. We have no choice. We have already "embarked."

What has happened in the world at large, and on the American campus in particular, now becomes clear. Those who hold a naturalistic outlook have challenged those who hold a Christian outlook to such a degree

[23] Harry E. Fosdick, *A Guide to Understanding the Bible,* New York: Harper and Brothers, 1938, p. xiv.

that in some instances Christians would seem to have become apologetic with regard to their faith, even to have had recourse to appeasement. Many a man of good will has abandoned the clear-cut Bible categories to seek refuge in vague forms of mysticism. The less we affirm, the less we offend, of course. But, then, to blur an issue is never a good way to dispose of it. We shall, therefore, come to grips in our next lecture with the challenge of naturalism to Christianity.

CHAPTER II

The Challenge of Naturalism

THE NATURALIST OUTLOOK

IN A MEDITATIVE MOOD one clear summer day, I remember wondering, on catching a flounder, what conception of the universe that flat fish might possibly have, reduced as it was to two dimensions.

Using our imagination, we can indeed think of a flounder as reading a learned paper at some congress of flounders. Amidst the approval of so many flat beings, he doubtless has no trouble in proving that, for all practical purposes, the universe has two dimensions. There is indeed a rumor noised abroad in the kelp that a brother flounder recently was caught by the mouth. Undergoing excruciating pain, he had the impression of being pulled up to some strange nowhere, out of the flounders' environment into a world so mysterious that no word or phrase of the flounder dialect could describe the experience. The glimpse he had of men as he dangled hopelessly, unable to breathe, the awesome fact that a noisy conversation was being carried on by fishermen who witnessed the catch, all this is, indeed, so impossible for a rescued flounder to relate, or even suggest, that I need not insist in order to make my point. Neither do I propose to overdo the case by introducing mention of a train passing by or of an airplane zooming overhead as the poorly hooked flounder slipped back into the ocean and so lived to tell the tale. Let us rather imagine that the rescued fish has by now been placed in the fishes' equivalent of an insane asylum until the day when the flounder in charge is hooked for good himself and lands in a frying pan rather impossible to imagine but none the less real.

Mind you, I am not joking. Rather would I share with you my impression that the world around us is teaching us in a thousand ways the abiding truth that no single creature in our deeply mysterious universe can ever claim to be the measure of all things. Some will object: "Well, we know that. We have read Kant's *Kritik der reinen Vernunft.*" I too have read that famous critique of pure reason, and I too thought I knew, just as many of us may say that we know we have to die some day, and yet we do not believe it. So also, while I probably would have passed a sophomore test on Kant's *Critique,* yet what he was driving at was not a real issue to me. It took my dog to make that issue alive.

I remember the occasion very well. We were vacationing in Southern California. War in Europe was felt to be imminent. Daladier had made his last appeal to Hitler, and Hitler repeatedly had lost his patience. Chamberlain was going to speak on the radio. As we had no radio in our cottage at that time, we did our listening in the family car. On that eventful evening I remember feeling my way to the car door in the garage, then falling back in the driver's seat, and turning on the radio. The little light of the dial was the only bright spot in the growing dusk. As I listened to Chamberlain's weary voice, I thought of what the war would mean. I had been through the last one. My boy already had volunteered and would be in this one. My old father was living in the east of France and already had known two German invasions. War . . . war . . . , a terrible war brewing. As I listened to Neville Chamberlain's voice, the whole tragedy became so real to me that I had the impression of actually being there. My mind was aflame with possible solutions. But in vain. I must have sighed deeply, as the weary voice continued. Suddenly I became aware that something warm had worked its way up under my arm and was now resting on my lap. It was my dog! His brown eyes, strangely sparkling in so much darkness, were alternately looking at me and at the spot of light on the radio dial.

Now, a dog is far better equipped for the perception of our world than a flat fish resting somewhere in the ocean, and is in every way much closer to our human situation. My dog had indeed some inkling of what was going on, and shared his master's anxiety. In his simple, wholehearted way he felt there was something wrong brewing somewhere. What was it? His obscure soul probably did not wander into anything like our realm of speculation. Just how far did it go, do you think? Certainly this "man's best friend" had no notion of Europe, or of war, or of our doomed civilization, or of possible danger to my boy and father in a far country. The world in which men live, and move, and have their being is a supernatural world to a dog. Let me add that my dog had penetrated it, or been penetrated by it, in the measure in which he loved me and I loved him. And we are very fond of each other.

You must believe me when I say that this experience was more of an eye-opener to me than the reading of many a learned treatise. To be sure, we ourselves conceive of a three-dimensional universe because we have three dimensions. Nay, we think with our whole body, and the rhythm of our thought has a great deal to do with that of our own organs and functions. Our vital activities shape themselves into rhythmic patterns because their forms begin with a rhythmic time originating in respiration and pulse. Our notions of orientation, the way in which we visualize shapes, depend on our various positions or attitudes, such as lying, standing, or sitting. These, in turn, are determined by our skeletal structure. Our notions of forms, the ways in which we experience motion in general, such as walking, running, and rolling, depend on our kinesthetic data. We could not have developed our abstract notions of deprivation and satisfaction, of attraction and repulsion, were it not for our digestive and generative functions. These functions, in their turn, are directly responsible for our ideas of growth, metamorphosis, and lifetime. So also the experience of sleeping and waking plays an important part in our sense of reality, duration, activity. Again, psychical perceptions of sense, emotion, ideation, and will are responsible for our sensations of light, sound, temperature, taste, smell; for notions such as pleasure and pain, desire and aversion, rest and unrest, attention and intention. Finally, as cause-chance and memory-thought construction are elaborations arising from so many elementary forms of the life of the mind, vital symbols reveal their psycho-physiological character. Now the dimensions of our thought are seen to be biographical and social as ever richer processes of metaphor and ideation unfold.

It is true, therefore, that we think with our whole body, this same organism being one with its environment. The awareness of this fact doubtless was at the origin of Jules Romains' creed of *unanimism,* just as in a more brutal rudimentary form it must have been, in part, at the origin of Hitler's bestial notion of totalitarianism. The fact is that each and every primitive cultural pattern proves to be totalitarian in character. Contemporary anthropology itself testifies to the dread of innovation in primitive society.

The *homo mensura* standardization of our experience causes us to measure the world in which we live in terms of ourselves. Thus our physical unities are set by our bodily dimensions. Hand, foot, and pace are all measures still in use in our day. We count according to the decimal system because we have ten fingers.

It should also be noted that when we thus use our own selves, however unconsciously, as the measure of our world, we are actually analyzing our own being. We make our human panorama of nature a mirror and reflection of ourselves. In fact we actually expand our nature as we assimilate its environment. Thus we find the inner self not only reflected in the outer world but coloring it and colored by it.

In a real way, then, we actually *are* the measure of all things, as old Protagoras used to say. Consequently, as we contemplate nature, as we read history, as we probe the remotest recesses of the human soul, as we consider and reconsider our human situation, we have the usual, and very natural, and, in a way, dismal feeling, of being unable, as it were, to jump outside our own shadow. "For what person knows a man's thoughts except the spirit of the man which is in him?"

When you come to think of it as a matter of fact, you realize that most of the misunderstandings between "believers" and "unbelievers," so-called, arise because both groups dispute the same ground with the same human organism. The human situation is the same for all of us; we witness the same universe, the same history, the same inner life. Nay, our physical make-up carries within itself the status of our own limitations. Being incapable of jumping outside our own shadow, we find we must actually cope with these limitations inherent in our human nature.

Now, the naturalists reason that since we have to be ourselves and to live with ourselves, we should be resigned to our lot. In this self-existent, self-operating, self-explanatory world of ours, they say, let us be satisfied to justify all that happens to us on natural grounds. In this universe without a purpose of which we may be aware, are we not merely incidental, at best normal happenings in the ordinary operations of nature? Or should we say simply that there is to the naturalist enough of a challenging vision in ethics, in the character and moral purpose which man will strive to achieve in a lifetime by means of custom or habit? Nay, allow me to insist for the sake of truth and intellectual honesty, a man may refuse to have anything to do with religion in general and the Christian faith in particular; he may repudiate them completely. His skepticism cannot be refuted within the limits acknowledged by naturalism, for naturalism in itself is perfectly sound. Let us face this fact and be tolerant accordingly.

THE CHRISTIAN OUTLOOK

Having thus made allowances for naturalism, we must further agree, however, that our inquiry also requires of us the conclusion that there is actually a hierarchy in our universe. There *are* levels. The world I contemplate—my world—is not the world of my dog, although this "man's best friend" be my constant companion. The world of my dog differs profoundly from that of a flounder. The hierarchy we have just suggested is evidence of instinctive, intellectual, and spiritual mutation, so that at a given level new vistas, almost undreamt of, will be opened.

We may be more specific still. Just as my dog one fateful evening came at one point into contact with a world to him supernatural but none the less real, it may be that at one point at least I myself may come into contact with a supernatural world. Just as the European drama escaped, for the most part, the understanding of my dog, a cosmic drama may unfold in the unknown without my having more than a poor inkling of it. To Karl Barth, divine revelation thus transcends human philosophy to the point of being comparable to a bolt in the blue; the "Word of God" is one thing, and the "word of man" is another thing. "It may be that the Word, the Word of God, which we ourselves shall never speak, has put on our weakness and unprofitableness so that *our* word in its very weakness and unprofitableness has become capable at least of being the mortal frame, the earthen vessel, of the Word of God." [1] Accordingly, we have been introduced to the "theology" of Karl Barth if we have heard him say *Veni, Creator Spiritus.* One thing is certain, namely, that the possibility of a divine revelation reaching us from a world which transcends our human situation may not be ruled out. This the naturalists must grant in their turn.

We may say even more than that. When the whole realm of experience proclaims the fact that the universe is actually a hierarchy providing for mutations undreamt of at a lower level, it would seem foolish on the part of man to rest satisfied in the conviction that *he* is the measure, the last word in perfection as it were. For that is what the humanistic, naturalistic attitude amounts to finally.

On this point at least the Bible contradicts man flatly, and actually calls such a smug attitude "foolishness," for "a fool," according to Scripture, is one who orders his life as though there were no God. The naturalist cannot be called mentally deficient by any stretch of the imagination. But even when assuming, however sincerely, an attitude of humility, he is seen

[1] Karl Barth, *The Word of God and the Word of Man,* translated by Douglas Horton, The Pilgrim Press, 1928, p. 216.

by the believer to be at heart arrogant. His sin is even said to be the very essence of sin, namely, self-sufficiency. And, as the *Theologia Germanica* has it, nothing burns in hell except self-will.

Christian philosophers, poets, artists, and cathedral builders have made their own the teaching of Paul, according to which disciples have received, not the spirit of this world, but the spirit which is of God, that they might know the things that are freely given to them of God. In these two verses of the First Letter to the Corinthians (2: 11, 12) they have found, as it were, a charter of knowledge. According to Thomas Aquinas we live on the borderline between the spiritual world and the world of sense experience —spiritual beings and yet engaged in matter—God-inspired, yet restricted by the limitations of matter. "We see and judge of all things in the light of the first truth, in so far as the light itself of our intellect . . . is nothing else than an impression of the first truth upon it . . .[2] If there existed in our souls a perfect image of God, as the Son is the perfect image of the Father, our mind would know God at once. But the image in our mind is imperfect . . ."[3] The hierarchy of creation thus reflected in the *Summa Theologica* rises in the domain of thought like the spire of a

[2] *Summa Theologica*, I, Q. 88, Art. 3. Reply obj. 1 (*Basic Writings of Saint Thomas Aquinas*, ed. by Anton C. Pegis, New York: Random House, 2 v. 1945, v. 1, 849).

[3] *Ibid.* Reply obj. 3. (*Ibid.*, 850).

cathedral piercing the blue mist of a glorious morning. The great Bible of stone, as Emile Mâle has called the medieval cathedral, suggests in turn a rich sense of participation with God. It speaks in type in the manner of the Old Testament preparing the way before the Gospel. Because the Synagogue could not read the harmony therein it was represented as blindfolded in the art of the thirteenth century.

The rapture of Thomas Aquinas in the Chapel of Saint Nicholas, as that of Dante at the end of *Paradiso*, is in a real way suggestive of a great vision of the universe caught by them that were born after the Spirit. So are the innumerable experiences of great Christians as they finally come to the realization that perfect freedom and bliss are to be found in captivity to the Divine. *Inquietum est cor nostrum, donec requiescat in te*—Our heart is uneasy until it resteth in Thee—as Augustine finally had to confess.

The achievement of this people of God should always be considered in the light of a same basic experience of which they are but the rationalization. Indeed, a tremendous amount of labor and exact science and thought went into the writing of Pascal's great page on the three orders of reality. To cite only one example, treating of the summation of numerical powers in his *Potestatum Numericarum Summa*, Pascal brought out, on the one hand, the wonderful connection which nature establishes between things in appearance the most contradictory, and on the other, showed that the lower orders are of no value, and therefore may be disregarded. For him, then, the infinity of mathematics was comparable to that of the soul. In the words of Professor Morris Bishop, Pascal actually "discovered a calculus of infinities more useful, perhaps, than that of Newton and Leibnitz. He found his certitude in that mysterious region where . . . geometrical propositions become emotions, like memory and joy." [4] At this point, the mathematician who, in his own field, outstripped Europe and inspired Leibnitz, the physicist who strictly conducted the most audacious experiments finally emerged into the light, to exalt his view of the universe in the language of a great religious poet. Allow me to quote here Pascal's essential passage on the hierarchy of the three orders of reality:

"All bodies, the firmament, the stars, the earth and its kingdoms, are not equal in value to the least feeling of love. This is of an order infinitely more exalted.

"From all bodies together, one cannot draw forth one tiny thought; that is impossible, and of another order. From all bodies and minds one cannot draw forth a feeling of true love; that is impossible, and of another order, supernatural." [5]

[4] Morris Bishop, *Pascal*, New York: Reynal and Hitchcock, 1936, p. 101.
[5] *Œuvres de Blaise Pascal*, "Les Grands Ecrivains de la France," Paris:

But, then, this final formulation of the three orders followed on the great night of November 23, 1654, when "from about half-past ten in the evening until about half-past twelve," Pascal saw in his room the Fire that is spoken of in the Bible, the Fire of the Flaming Bush "that burned and did not burn out." Furthermore, I have now come to the conclusion that the completion of that page on the three orders is contemporaneous with the *Mystère de Jésus*. In his retreat at Port Royal, Pascal, having watched with Jesus, actually heard the Saviour say to him:

"Console thyself; thou wouldst not be seeking Me, hadst thou not already found Me.

"I was thinking of thee in My agony; I have shed such and such drops of blood for thee."

And Blaise had then uttered these supreme words of consecration:

"Lord, I give Thee all." [6]

He was now aware of the fact that, in his own words: "Jesus will be in agony until the end of the world; we must not sleep during all that time." [7] On reaching such heights in the *Mystère de Jésus*, we

---

Hachette, 14 v., v. 14, (*Pensées* iii, ed. by L. Brunschvicg, Sect. xii, frag, 793), 233.

[6] *Œuvres*, op. cit., vi. 13, (*Pensées* ii, Sect. vii, frag. 553), 438, 439.

[7] *Ibid.*, 435.

would not draw nigher, for the place whereon we now stand is holy ground.

And yet it is from this holy ground, from this supernatural order, that we now behold the world of men and affairs. What I am saying is that this world of the Christian believer is a world of his own, which has its unity, its basis in the solid facts of experience and history, its full justification in the world of scholarship, just as we have found it to be the case with the world of the naturalist. But to the onlooker the two worlds look like the same world.

A MATTER OF INTERPRETATION

It is true, then, that all human beings dispute the same ground of experience with the same organism. As that situation becomes increasingly clear, those dominated by what Paul has labeled "the spirit of man" are found to possess a unit and method of measurement which differ markedly from those of the "Godly-spirited." We find we have to cope with two widely divergent sets of people. Together, they are confronted with the same reality—nay, with the same Bible and the same Christ. But our question is now twofold: in this world within the Bible, shall man be the measure, or shall God be the measure?

The fact that this question in its wider implications actually goes beyond the realm of Christianity is likely to render our discussion more serene.

The history of philosophy teaches clearly that two tendencies dominate the thinking of men: that of Protagoras, for whom, as we have already stated, man is the measure of all things; that of Plato, who, searching for a better form of government in the Fourth Book of his *Laws,* wonders who will take the measure of the same, and offers God as the answer: "In our eyes God will be the measure of all things, in the highest degree—a degree much higher than is any 'man' they talk of." [8] A clear allusion on Plato's part to the dictum of Protagoras.

We must realize at the outset that in this, our common realm of experience, the results of our spiritual quest are presupposed in our starting point and in our method. It is indeed a question of *either-or*. If man be the measure, then we may expect to deal with mechanists, who reduce everything to the most elementary forms of existence, with empirical idealists, who reduce everything to the most elementary forms of understanding; with monists and materialists, who persist in explaining the superior by the inferior, all of them making of man an idol which they are sure in due time to reclaim more or less clearly and consciously.

If, on the other hand, God be the measure, then we may expect to find in direct contrast people who

[8] The Loeb classical library, *Plato,* with an English translation, ix *Laws,* by R. G. Bury, in 2 v., v. 1, 295.

gradually find themselves raised up to the notion of a self-justified and self-sufficient reason, men who then grope for some manifestation of the living God in nature, in history, and in their own lives and souls. In this effort God helps them to understand their own soul; their soul in turn helps them to understand nature and to recognize throughout the Bible the Redeeming One at work in and through the stuff of history. As the Editor of *Theology Today* puts it: In this Book, God meets men face to face. The Bible is essentially

"the record of God's revelation to mankind, the abiding witness to the fact that He has spoken. *God has spoken*. This is the message of the Bible. There is a word from the Lord, an authoritative account of His relation to the world and to man. The eternal silence has been broken. Light has shone upon the mystery of man's life. A divine answer has been given to the problem of his sin. The hidden God has become manifest in a new order of life. The one stupendous fact with which the Bible deals is that God has spoken by saving deeds and enlightening words. The Book is the record of His self-communication at different times and through diverse agents. It is thereby, in a wholly unique sense, the Word of God." [9]

But then there are those who have "eyes to see, and do not see." To many a man of letters, the Bible is only a monument of English prose, and we have al-

[9] John A. Mackay, in *Theology Today*, v. 3, nr. 2, July, 1946, 145.

ready quoted the penetrating remarks of T. S. Eliot on this subject.

As we might expect, the Bible has many illustrations of this great issue; yet the most striking of them all seems to be a scene of the Crucifixion. You will recall that Jesus suffers His last agony between two thieves, one on the right hand and one on the left. Having looked at Jesus, then at himself, the repentant thief felt convicted of sin in the Light of a holy Saviour and proceeded to confess his sin in godly sorrow, and to pray to his Lord in faith, hope, and charity. Thereupon, the good thief was forgiven, and received in a hallowed moment the divine assurance of salvation. In the case of the other thief, we witness the eternal tragedy of perdition, as, in the words of the Gospel account, one of the malefactors who were being hanged railed at him, saying, "Are you not the Christ? Save yourself and us!"

I have pondered over that scene again and again. We are all aware that ours is the era of a critical approach to the historical and literary problems of the Bible. More especially are we warned against retouching the portrait which objective scholarship paints of Jesus, lest we be "found guilty of trying to correct the Wisdom of God by the wisdom of men." [10] And yet, out of a group of theologians who have restored the

[10] Walter M. Horton in his Foreword to J. W. Bowman's *The Intention of Jesus,* Philadelphia: The Westminster Press, 1943, p. vii.

scene of the Crucifixion through the same tested
methods of investigation, some will take their stand
beside the repentant thief; others will find themselves
on the side of his fellow, unrepentant, and say to Jesus
in their own way: "Are you not the Christ? Save
yourself and us!" Why? Because at every crossroad
in life their naturalism calls for objective tests.[11]

The real issue, then, is not a matter of scholarship.
Indeed, a reverent approach to the New Testament's
literary and historical problems is as legitimate and
proves as useful as scientific investigations in the realms
of physics and astronomy. It is not condemnable in
itself. The time has come for Fundamentalists to realize that it is as bad to denounce the New Testament
scholar as it is for short-sighted men in the past to
have denounced and condemned as heretical the system of Copernicus or to have forced the abjuration of
Galileo. The fact is that we should, in this connection,
carefully ponder Galileo's treatise on *The Authority of
Scripture,* clarifying the relation between physical science and Holy Writ. But more about this later.

It is humiliating, in a way, that such a book as *A
History of the Warfare of Science with Theology in
Christendom* [12] need ever have been written. We
repeat that the same ground of investigation is being

[11] Emile Cailliet, *Pascal, Genius in the Light of Scripture,* Philadelphia:
The Westminster Press, 1945, p. 362.
[12] by Andrew D. White, New York: D. Appleton & Co., 1913, 2 v.

faced today, as before, by the same human nature, although it makes a great difference according to whether this same human nature has been redeemed or not. Therefore, as we carry on research, our ambition should be to make use of the very best in scientific equipment. I agree with Professor John W. Bowman, whose views I do not always share, that "the proverbial 'ostrich' attitude toward truth, arrived at by whatever means and from whatever quarter, when adopted by the devotees of any faith, will in the end spell disaster to that faith." [13]

No, the real issue in this, our spiritual quest, is not one of scholarship. Tested methods of investigation being the same on both sides, the final decision proves to be a matter of interpretation dependent on the orientation of the scholar's whole life and thought. Those who claim that the Christian faith has been dealt the final death blow by the rise of a pagan naturalism would do well to turn to the very latest edition of *Who's Who in America*. There they would find an imposing array of qualified authorities willing to admit that the news of their death is being somewhat exaggerated, to use a current and somewhat worn-out joke.

[13] *The Intention of Jesus, op. cit.,* p. 4.

CHAPTER III

The Dilemma of Christian Scholarship

HEBREW RELIGION AND GREEK THOUGHT

HAVING THUS BROUGHT the issue to a head, we realize that we now have on our hands what proves to be the dilemma of Christian scholarship, since revealed truth must needs be integrated through human reason. J. S. Whale put it in a nutshell when, in his excellent 1940 lectures in the University of Cambridge, he admitted that "If Greek thought creates a difficulty for religion, Hebrew religion creates a difficulty for thought." [1]

Thus we have to face the fact that our Western culture has adapted itself to Greek ways of thinking. Only too much so, for the verb "to adapt" is often too close for comfort to the verb "to adopt."

And so it happens that, as we face it here today, the problem is no longer to discover how the Christian faith may best be formulated so as not to create problems for Greek thought; for this would smack of appeasement as you readily see. Rather the problem is

[1] *Christian Doctrine, op. cit.,* p. 57.

to find out how certain vague and lifeless forms of Christian mysticism may be worked back to their home, to undergo first-aid treatment with a view to final recovery.

The ultimate reference of these forms to the Messianic categories which were fulfilled in Jesus is essential if the biblical revelation is to mean anything. For a mere 'mystical' experience is not the same thing as Christianity by a far cry. In the words of the late J. Gresham Machen, "A gospel independent of history is a contradiction in terms. The Christian Gospel means, not a presentation of what always has been true, but a report of something new—something that imparts a totally different aspect to the situation of mankind." [2]

Ever since Schweitzer published his famous book, *The Quest for the Historical Jesus,* forcing the eschatological outlook back into the categories of the New Testament, the false security of a Christian mysticism at ease in an Hellenistic context of thought has been greatly disturbed. Soon the Fourth Gospel whose roots had been found to draw nourishments from Greek soil, revealed its essentially Jewish texture and background, until it was discovered to have been written much earlier than generally had been assumed. Neither could Paul be denounced any longer as the "gratuitous so-

[2] J. Gresham Machen, *Christianity and Liberalism,* New York: Macmillan, 1923, p. 121.

phisticator" who had changed the Galilean idyl into a cosmic drama of redemption, thus substituting belief *in* Jesus Christ for the simple faith *of* Jesus. As a result, the death and resurrection of the Messiah became once more a stumbling block to the Greek, as it had always been a scandal to the Jew.

We are told that passing through Antioch, Paul went into the synagogue on the sabbath day and sat down; but after the reading of the Law and the Prophets, he was asked by the rulers to give a word of exhortation. As we read his proclamation in the thirteenth chapter of The Acts of the Apostles we are impressed by its utterly Hebrew character. Starting from the heritage of Israel, it leads up to the resurrection of the dead, which is then fully expounded in the framework of Old Testament eschatological categories. Now, as Paul goes on his way with Barnabas, the people beg that these things might be told them on the next Sabbath. Not only do the converts follow our two missionaries and urge them to continue in the grace of God, but on the next Sabbath, we are told, the whole city gathers to hear them. The fact that they are finally driven out of the district by jealous Jews does not affect our argument.

Later, Paul, having met in the market place at Athens some Epicurean and Stoic philosophers, is invited to tell them at the Areopagus what this new teaching is which he presents. As long as he talks to them of the "unknown" God worshiped at one of their altars, they listen to him; but as soon as he comes to the subject of the resurrection of the dead, some mock, and others say, "We will hear you again about this." Only a few join him and believe, among whom two are named.

Notice that never again do we find Paul engaging in philosophical arguments. To him theology must simply be the exposition of the Messianic hope of Israel as fulfilled by Jesus in the fulness of time; and just as Paul was followed by only a few of his listeners at the Areopagus, he will be followed whole-heartedly only by a few throughout the history of Christianity—such as Tertullian in the early third century, Bernard de Clairvaux in the twelfth century, and the Reformers in the sixteenth. Plotinus and Porphyry will prove to be more popular with the sons of Greece, down to Spinoza and Hegel.

Not only are the Christians divided among themselves but they are also divided *within* themselves. Even Augustine provides us with a good example of the case in point. At the end of Book VII in his *Confessions* you will find that he had to learn to differentiate between the prologue of John's Gospel and "the falsehood of Plotinus." In the twentieth chapter he tells how he rejoiced that he had proceeded from Plato to the Holy Scriptures, and not the reverse. Some of our theologians, who seem, indeed, to be doing the reverse, might do well to turn to the hallowed pages of that learned Christian. The twenty-first chapter exults in what Augustine found in the sacred books, "which are not to be found in Plato." [3]

When a reassertion of the Greek way of thinking confronted the cloistered wisdom of medieval Christianity with the thesis of Aristotle and of his Greek and Arabian commentators, the disciples of Augustine, among others, were caught unprepared. What did they know of Greek philosophy? It took the genius of a Thomas Aquinas to bring about a conciliation between the teaching of the Church and that of an Aristotle expurgated to suit the occasion. Moreover the agreement was bought at a price. In order to come to terms with Aristotle, Aquinas had to come to grips with the disciples of Augustine, using against them the very weapons wrought of yore by Aristotle himself against Plato.

Yet Greek thought and Hebrew religion remained strange bedfellows. After a period of decadence in scholasticism, an impatient Hellenism reasserted its claim. In all justice to scholasticism, it must be emphasized that the ranks of its doctors had been sadly depleted by the Black Death. The reassertion of the Greek outlook we have come to call the Renaissance. This very name implied scorn for the medieval civil-

[3] *The Confessions of St. Augustine* translated and annotated by J. G. Pilkington, M. A., with Biographical Introduction, New York: Liveright Publishing Company, 1943, pp. 157, 158, 159.

ization on the part of the Age of Enlightenment. To the eighteenth-century mind, 'Gothic' meant "barbarian." Should you look through the large *Encyclopédie* of Diderot and d'Alembert you would soon find out that according to many an article therein, the source of such "barbarism" is said to be in the main none other than Palestinian. With that point of view the *Encyclopédie* came to revise the history of the origins of our Western civilization, even at the cost of great linguistic heresies.

But, then, watch for a reassertion of the Hebrew-Christian point of view as the Renaissance scholar John Calvin parts ways with the Renaissance, more specifically with the "Do as ye will" credo of the humanist Rabelais, for that constituted the charter of man's self-sufficiency, in other terms, the very essence of sin.

Consider in the light of the above statement Calvin's *Christianæ Religionis Institutio*. This monumental work is not, as generally believed (especially by people who criticize without having even read the *Institutio*), a treatise on predestination. Predestination occupies only one chapter (VIII) in seventeen; and this section, like the rest, is, we may well believe, in Calvin's book only because he found it in Scripture. What Calvin attempted to do in this *Institutio* essentially is this: after careful comparison of the Bible's teachings and the commentaries and writings of the Fathers and Doctors of the Church, he set out to disentangle the

Holy Writ from the tremendous mass of literature which threatened to engulf it. The purpose, again, was to release the pure crystal of Biblical truth from the common alloy that had been heaped upon it, and to mount every gem in the restored Scriptural framework to which it belonged.

Let God alone speak to us, this was the cry of a great Reformer, who, as we have just seen, had only a short time previously been one of the leading men of the Renaissance. The Reformation, then, can be called essentially a re-Judaization of culture, just as the Renaissance was a reassertion of Greek thought. Yet conscientious consideration of a man like John Calvin suggests that there can be such a thing as a Christian scholar. And if genuine Christian scholarship was possible in the days of the Renaissance it must surely be possible in our time. Nay, let us take stock of our tradition of Christian culture, of its amazing wealth in masterpieces that cover every realm of human endeavor. Let us realize what faith, what circumstances made such productions possible. Above all, let us *learn* from the imposing array of evangelical men who were the salt of our Christian civilization in all the lands, and we will in due time glow with a true enthusiasm, and, in the end, behold a new Age of Christian Humanism.

Does this mean, however, that it will ever be possible for an existing culture to annex Christianity on its own terms? The best way to answer this question is to look at the record for precedents.

AUGUSTINE EXPOSES PELAGIUS

At the beginning of the fifth century, the British theologian Pelagius, coming to Rome on a visit, was shocked at the low tone of morality prevalent in the holy city. What could be done about it? The weak were making an excuse of their weakness; but to Pelagius it seemed evident that the Augustinian doctrine of a depravity permeating the whole of human nature could not meet the actual need. What men wanted, Pelagius thought, was a firm consciousness of their actual powers, an exaltation of their will. If I ought, I can, such became the message of this well-meaning reformer, in opposition to Augustine's, which stressed the bondage of will in man's fallen nature. As is often the case, expediency brought Pelagius to a new formulation of Biblical doctrine. In the long run, he came to deny original sin. In his eyes there no longer existed such a thing as man's inability to meet the requirements of righteousness. What, then, was the need for the Gospel of new birth and regeneration by the Holy Spirit? What was the need indeed for Jesus Christ Himself? Augustine strongly objected to the new tenets, and Pelagius, after some hesitation, came to another compromise: he maintained the availability of Divine aid, of grace offered. But, according to his point of view, in the work of salvation the initiative had passed to man.

Such "Semi-Pelagianism" was contested by Augustine, and it led him to write in answer to Pelagius' book *De Natura* his own work, entitled *De Natura et Gratia,* in which he commended the former's zeal for human liberty and moral responsibility, but also went further into the details of the controversy. From statements about infant baptism, Augustine, carried along by the demands of a rebounding theological dispute, pursued over a period of twelve years speculation on such issues as the sanctification of marriage, the Manichean conception of the flesh, and other doubtful questions, thereby permitting himself to be driven from exaggeration to exaggeration, often into regrettable inconsistency. Such is bound to be the fate of even the greatest Christian doctors when they allow themselves to become involved in naturalistic utterances. That outcome should not, however, detract in any way from our profound admiration for Augustine, author of an immortal testimony as a Christian in the style of "the greatest man that ever wrote in Latin," which we find in *The City of God* and the *Confessions.* But so far as the Christian testimony is concerned, we must turn to the Apostle Paul, and finally to the Lord Himself, in order to gain the full measure of Augustine. We seem to learn more and more that the human commentary is ever to be read in close contact with the Biblical text. Theory can be studied only in the context of a statement of fact.

LUTHER SHATTERS A DREAM OF ERASMUS

Erasmus, prince of all humanists, a charming moralist and a diverting Latinist, dreamed of building up a Catholicism which would be strong enough and sure enough of itself to tolerate the maximum freedom for the human mind. The medium of expression for such a Catholicism was to be Latin, promoted to the rank of universal language for the élite.

Soon the Jesuits were to form the majority at the Council of Trent, where they exerted considerable influence and at the same time organized a new form of teaching in their schools, which was based on the study of the ancient classics.

While Erasmus was nursing his dream of universal humanism, Luther was rediscovering the Bible, which, translated by him into the native tongue, eventually became the textbook of a nation. As this movement spread throughout the Western world, Christians who came to know the standards of the Bible first-hand, were put in a position to pass judgment on every form of compromise between the Church and the lay world. The popes of those times, among them Julius II and Leo X, appeared, in the luxury that surrounded them, to be essentially promoters of a pagan Renaissance.

Pascal Shows Up The Jesuits

That kind of a rôle might be praiseworthy in itself, as it surely was of great service to culture; but was it not also in some measure idolatrous? Did it not grant to Cæsar *more* than was required? Indeed, did it not grant Cæsar most of what belonged to God?

Again, one could say that the spirit of compromise in the Jesuits might have been praiseworthy in intent, and charity would have us place such an interpretation on its various manifestations.

However, a great Bible-made man, Blaise Pascal, appeared on the scene as the Augustine of the seventeenth century, to denounce vehemently the "Semi-Pelagianism" of Molina the Jesuit, and, indeed, to denounce the new compromising tenets of all Molinists. In his *Lettres Provinciales,* which were to inaugurate the grand tradition of modern French prose, Pascal exposed what he clearly saw to be another heresy.

Once again new concepts of theology appeared to be dictated by a peculiar conception of morality, and such a conception in turn, by a deep-seated desire to address contemporaries in a language that would entice them to swell the Christian fold. Yet again these dreams came to naught.

Once more the dividing line was distinctly drawn between what belongs to God and the things that are Cæsar's. Unerringly, Pascal and his Jansenist friends found their way back to Augustine, to Paul, to the Christ.

KIERKEGAARD ECHOES PASCAL

Let this part of our agreement be summed up by Kierkegaard, the Danish Pascal. In his *Journals,* as well as in many an issue of his pamphlet *The Instant,* he echoes in his own way the Pascal of the *Lettres Provinciales* and of the *Comparaison des Chrétiens des Premiers Temps avec Ceux d'Aujourd'hui.* A fascinating and most unusual comparison could be drawn between the two testimonies. Let us hope that some day the task will be undertaken. For the present we must be satisfied with borrowing from Kierkegaard's *Journals* this pungent summing-up of the point made above. Man's knavish interest, Kierkegaard proclaims,

"consists in creating millions and millions of Christians, the more the better, all men if possible; for thus the whole difficulty of being a Christian vanishes, being a Christian and being a man amount to the same thing, and we find ourselves where paganism ended.

"Christendom has mocked God and continues to mock Him—just as if to a man who is a lover of nuts, instead of bringing one nut with a kernel, we were to bring him tons and millions . . . of empty nuts, and then make this show of our zeal to comply with his wish." [4]

[4] XI² A 390. Cf. *Attack upon "Christendom"* by Søren Kierkegaard, translated by Walter Lowrie, Princeton University Press, 1944, p. 156.

The fourth issue of Kierkegaard's *Instant*—among others—then gives the gist of the entire argument in the heading, "In 'Christendom' all are Christians; when all are Christians, the New Testament *eo ipso* does not exist, yea, it is impossible." [5]

It is an amazing spectacle in the history of Christianity to see how any attempt by an existing culture to annex Christianity on its own terms inevitably will bring about a reaction of Christianity against that culture. This is another way of stating the fact of God's sovereignty over human culture, which will prove to be the Alpha and the Omega of any attempt to bring about the truly Biblical humanism we are advocating throughout these lectures.

"THE GODS THAT HAVE NOT MADE THE HEAVENS AND THE EARTH"

We have not been saying that the Greeks were not religious. Such a statement would amount to illiteracy. Why, the whole Greek countryside, its groves and streams, its hills and the blue Mediterranean sky over them, were teeming with spirits suggested by local myths and wonderful stories. The rustic life thrived on nature spirits, as did the metropolitan life with its gods and goddesses. Even great gods of mythology, such as Apollo, changed in nature and priesthood according to whether they were worshiped in Delos or

---

[5] *Attack upon "Christendom," op. cit.,* p. 149.

in Delphi. The Homeric epics were born in such a world. So were the dramas of Sophocles and even the dialogues of Plato. In due time, Orphism came to be expressed in terms of Pythagorean philosophy.

To the Greeks, the world was "full of gods"; but these were parts of nature. Nature itself was divine. According to Plato's *Timæus,* the celestial bodies were "visible" gods, and even for the matter-of-fact biologist, Aristotle, the gods were to be found in the most insignificant living being. That is why it seemed a pity to the scholastics to refrain from making use of such views and conveying the notion of God's omnipresence in His creation.

But, then, the Greek universe was not a *created* universe, while the idea of creation is one of the main features of the Biblical outlook. In the Bible little scope is given to mere mysticism, but instead there is a magnificent Hebrew imagery suggesting the *reality* of God, differing considerably from sheer philosophical monotheism. And just as there is in the entire Bible no instance of a process of logic to prove the being of God, so is there no effort at a scientific demonstration of the newness of the world. As Thomas Aquinas has shown in his *Summa Theologica,* the fact that "the world did not always exist we hold by faith alone: it cannot be proved demonstratively. . . . Neither can the newness of the world be demonstrated from the efficient cause, which acts by will. For the will of God cannot be investigated by reason." [6] Therefore, there can be no useful debate on this question, from the agnostic viewpoint of modern philosophy. It would not lead anyone anywhere.

Let us rather learn from The Letter to the Hebrews: "By faith we understand that the world was created by the word of God, so that what is seen was made out of things which do not appear"(2:3). Neither can modern science disagree, since it has nothing to say on the subject. What the Hebrew-Christian revelation does, in fact, is to project a new light on a realm of thought in which the contemporary physicist finds himself entirely in the dark. Again, this revealed description of existence will be for the Christian student something which adequately expresses his adoring sense of a Sovereign God and his own dependence on God.

As the well-read and tolerant man he should be, the Christian student will appreciate the faith of the ancient Greeks, its sincerity, its grandeur, and the poetic charm of its naturism. He will appreciate the fact that while our modern drama deserted the cathedral for the marketplace, and eventually for a pagan structure, Æschylus took tragedy from the marketplace and brought it to the shrine of Dionysus on the slope of the Acropolis below the Parthenon. He will

[6] *Summa Theologica*, I. Q. 46. Art. 2. (*Basic Writings of Saint Thomas Aquinas, op. cit.*, v. I, 453.)

not be sparing in his praise of the Fundamentalist Sophocles, one of the most religious men of Athens, who, although upset by his contemporaries' unbelief in oracles, yet was willing to learn from these same contemporaries. The Christian student will also appreciate the fact that while formalism too often has parched the sensitiveness of Christian disciples rather indifferent to the ways in which God clothes the fields in grass, scholars such as Thaddæus Zielinski, in his *Religion of Ancient Greece,* still exult with contagious enthusiasm, in a life infused with spirit and divinity, such as glows in the fragrant grove and in the ripening grace of the garden. At this point, our student will even excuse the Greek scholar if he exaggerates in calling a religion which denies nature any feeling of gratitude a form of poison.

The Christian student will acknowledge with genuine admiration the truly religious inspiration of Hellenistic metaphysics. In saying this we are referring not merely to the one who has deserved to be called the "divine" Plato, especially for such works as the half-mythological *Timæus* in which his "Absolute God" took the form of a demiurge endowed with providential concern and will. We also mean Aristotle himself, thinking especially of the Twelfth Book of his *Metaphysics,* the most restrained, yet the most moving hymn ever dedicated by the Greek mind to the One who moves all things through love. The Seventh Book of Aristotle's *Eudemian Ethics* is less known perhaps in this connection; yet what a tribute it pays (VII, xiv) to the divine in us!

When the Christian student attains with Aristotle to the concept of *theoria,* as to the pure contemplation of a contemplative God, he knows that sharing in this contemplation would make him happy as "none of the other animals is happy, since they in no way share in this contemplation." [7] Yet he knows also that such an attitude is necessarily esthetic, and does not bring him so far as to be on speaking terms with any divine Reality. The charm does not make communication possible. Indeed, any thought of relationship would be as disturbing at this juncture as a clumsy movement by a photographer aiming at a fixed star many thousands of light-years away.

When, finally, the Christian student sees a materialist like Epicurus paying tribute to the gods, he comes to realize that such speculations as those of Greek philosophy on the "nature of the gods" cannot be reconciled with the Hebrew-Christian revealed truth unless a high price be paid for such a feat. While the Bible speaks of God's creation, the Greek divinities had simply nothing to do with the mechanical processes of nature. Indeed, Greek philosophy, once freed from mythology and obsolete cosmological connotations, spoke of transformism.

[7] *Ethica Nicomachea, op. cit.,* X, 8, 1178b.

Aristotle set out to prove in his *Physics* that the world is eternal. This, in a way, was an improvement over the other philosophers, some of whom were satisfied with statements on the eternity of matter. The plain fact is, any compromise with matter appeared to all of them as incompatible with the metaphysical perfection of God. On the other hand, the Jews could not compromise on the notion of creation *ex nihilo,* which excluded the Greek idea of the eternity of matter.

To the Greeks, then, everything came about by transformation, the transformation of something into something else. In this manner the Aristotelian soul became the realization of potentialities in which the universe manifested its existence. Hence, the mood of panpsychism, which, in our day, has reappeared in Bergson's *élan vital* and in Whitehead's notion of "Process and Reality." And thus we find Whitehead's first article of faith formulated as follows: "We know nothing beyond this temporal world and the formative elements which jointly constitute its character. The temporal world and its formative elements constitute for us the all-inclusive universe." [8]

This quotation is taken from the Lowell Lectures, 1926, entitled, interestingly enough, *Religion in the Making.* Now, Whitehead sees religion to be "in the

[8] Alfred North Whitehead, *Religion in the Making,* Lowell Lectures, 1926, New York: The Macmillan Company, 1926, p. 90.

making" because in its attempt to evolve "notions which strike more deeply into the root of reality" progress in truth is at the same time progress in "truth of science and truth of religion." [9] Again, such progress reaches its final principle in the conviction that *"there is a wisdom in the nature of things, from which flow our direction of practice,* and our possibility of the theoretical analysis of fact." [10] A naturalistic creed of this sort sounds rather weird in our atomic age! It may be that natural science is called on to provide us with a new organized system of thought destined in many respects to play the part of theology, yet Christian theology, from the Apostle Paul to Reinhold Niebuhr, tallies far better than the naturism of Whitehead with available data on our human situation.

We admit that a religion may be said to be "in the making" when the best god it can evolve is one "who is the ground antecedent to transition," who "must include all possibilities of physical value conceptually, thereby holding the ideal forms apart in equal, conceptual realization of knowledge." [11] Another great scientist was closer to the truth when, during a night of humble meditation and prayer over his open Bible, he received the final assurance that the true God, the

[9] *Ibid*, p. 131.

[10] *Ibid.*, p. 143. Italics ours.
Compare with editorial, "Is God Process or Person?" *The Christian Century*, lxiv 5, January 29, 1947, 134-137.

[11] *Ibid.*, p. 153.

Living God, is the "God of Abraham, God of Isaac, God of Jacob, not of the philosophers and scholars." [12] The vital affirmation undergirding the entire Bible is that of the *reality* of this Living God. Consequently, we know the basic truth that matters, and our thinking should proceed from that known principle. This being the case, one must also vindicate the old Aramaic verse of Jeremiah, which reads: "The gods that have not made the heavens and the earth, *even* they shall perish from the earth, and from under these heavens" (10:11). Let the Christian therefore steer clear of the tragedy that befell Hamlet, the tragedy of un-reality.

What may be said to be "in the making" is the individual and historical interpretation of revealed truth; it is the language spoken by the faith of a particular person and of a particular time. We further agree that the process according to which revealed truth is received and finally assimilated by the individual is an extremely complex one. In this connection Emil Brunner speaks of "truth as an encounter" (*Wahrheit als Begegnung*).[13] Yet the whole point at issue is that God has not left us in the dark. *He has spoken.*

[12] *Œuvres de Blaise Pascal, op. cit.,* v. 12, 4.
[13] Title of a short volume translated by Amandus W. Loos under the title *The Divine-Human Encounter,* Philadelphia: The Westminster Press, 1943.

If our religious life should be left without the body of truth revealed or proclaimed in our Hebrew-Christian tradition, we should understand what Bunyan meant when he saw the discouraging clouds of confusion hang over the Valley of the Shadow of Death. Anyone who has attended a student forum on religion knows how soon the point may be reached when nothing is taken for granted any longer. If we should try to live without the Word that God has spoken, we may even be left with little more than a confusing psychic experience of the dynamism of nature reflected in our soul. Nay, we may even become susceptible to the most extravagant interpretations of such an experience.

I for one cannot echo Dr. McGiffert's exultation as he hails the fact that divine immanence proved to be the characteristic doctrine of the nineteenth century, although it did make faith "infinitely easier than it was under the old regime," [14] as Dr. Fosdick puts it. Panpsychism of that variety leads inevitably to certain "unformulated experiences," such as the one undergone by a college junior and suggested by Professor Gordon W. Allport of the Harvard Psychology Department. It follows, quoted in the student's own words: "I remember once a few years ago I had gone for a walk alone and came to the top of a hill. It

[14] Harry E. Fosdick, *The Modern Use of the Bible,* New York: The Macmillan Company, 1924, p. 267.

was a beautiful day, and I stretched out my arms, and had a most indescribable feeling of fulness and completeness. I remember I said out loud something that sounds foolish now. I said, 'I know all, I see all, I am all.' " To which the professor answered approvingly, "That was a typical mystical experience." [15] And so it truly was. And so were the ravings of the Sibyl above her pit at Cumes, whose trance was so powerfully suggested by Vergil. So also were the "intuitions" of Hitler in the midst of Wagnerian paraphernalia and pagan myth. Buchenwald was the direct outcome of such "primitive" mysticism. Any such mysticism is to be feared in an age in which totalitarianism lurks as an ever-present danger. Totalitarianism is a primitive feature, as you know. Already contemporary authors are suggesting models of myths, which, mind you, our military authorities may find any day painted in red on the walls of the caves they are mapping out all over the land, just in case . . .

And thus it comes about that our speculations on Christian scholarship, far from being held aloof as mere fancies of the mind, may turn out to be strangely relevant in the present world of men and affairs.

[15] Gordon W. Allport, *The Roots of Religion,* published by the National Council of the Protestant Episcopal Church, New York, pp. 15, 16. In all justice to Professor Allport, quoted above, it should be added that his acknowledgment of the said experience was but a way of drawing the student within the area of revealed Christianity.

Is There a Meaning to History?

From the Stoic's viewpoint a wise man was not concerned with time. How could he be, in view of the Greek conception of God? In the context of Aristotle's *Meteors* (I, ii, 2, 339) the tumult of meaningless cycles of history glittered endlessly. Man knew that his fate was bound in everyday circumstances in accordance with astrological processes. At the lower level of popular mythology it may become possible, according to Jocasta's words in *Œdipus King,* to "cheat Apollo of his will." [16] The very gods "that did not make the heavens or the earth" were competing with man. As Herodotus saw it, they were wont to dock everything that stood out. On every side, therefore, was excess dangerous, coming as it did either from gods that were jealous of men's success, or from man himself if he were tempted to go astray. In the long run the good life must needs be formulated in terms of the humanistic doctrine of the mean, and sophistication alone saved man from fabulous forms of doom. As we know, sophistication in many subtle, insidious ways would sap of all its unique character the old Athenian tradition, which had men paid to argue for victory rather than for truth. As a satire on this very disease

---

[16] Sophocles, *Œdipus King of Thebes,* v.v. 721, 722, translated by Gilbert Murray, Oxford University Press, 1911, p. 42.

Aristophanes wrote that revealing comedy, *The Clouds.*

Now, contrast for a moment such concepts with the Hebrew-Christian notion of history. Even the individual's life history is included in the framework of a created universe distinct from its Creator yet utterly dependent on Him. For that Creator is still at work at the roaring loom of events; nay, using history as a means of Self-Disclosure, He is ever at work. History, thus unfolded, is a tale either of obedience or of would-be rebellion on the part of men and nations. In *De Civitate Dei* Augustine would give full scope to the implications of this purposeful Hebrew-Christian concept of time. Indeed, it is to this concept that we owe the best of our secular philosophy of history, securalized though it was by Voltaire in his *Essai sur les Mœurs* and by Condorcet in his *Esquisse d'un Tableau Historique des Progrès de l'Esprit Humain.*

As the Creator breaks in on eternity in a meaningful intervention, that is, as time begins, it becomes possible for the individual creature to refer his own life to his Creator. Thus in the Tenth Book of the *Confessions* we find this prayer: "O Thou my true life, my God, I will pass even beyond this power of mine which is called memory.[17] . . . I will pass beyond it, that I may proceed to Thee." Incidentally,

[17] *The Confessions of St. Augustine, op. cit.,* p. 238.

Augustine's magnificent analysis of the process of conscience and memory [18] turns out to have blazed the trail for those of Freud and Bergson; indeed, we may truly consider Augustine to be the founder of modern psychology. So true is it that knowledge concerning human nature as seen through the Bible tallies with the facts as we, at our best, know them.

We have now left far behind those Greek divinities, be they the gods of popular religion or the atomistic material gods of learned philosophy, which, in any event, paid no attention to man. What could *they* have in common with my Creator, my Redeemer, the Master of my soul who knows all my comings in and my goings forth?

The fact remains that all attempts at a compromise between Judaism and Hellenism under the general heading of scholasticism have had dire results in at least two connections. Not only has the historical figure of Jesus been lost in metaphysical and cosmological speculations, but the conclusions reached have proven unacceptable to our modern nominalism. Thus experimental science has shown that the so-called "essences" or "substances" were, in fact, the definition, not of given realities, but of their names.

[18] Cf. especially Book 10, ch. 8-19.

CHAPTER IV

A Charter for the Christian Scholar

THE OUTLOOK OF THE SCIENTIST

WHEN EVERYTHING has been said and done, when "the gods that have not made the heavens and the earth" have been dispelled by the nominalism of modern thought, the basic affirmation which we inherit from Greek wisdom is that the simplest of our statements, even in the world of axioms, must remain beyond verification. Mathematicians will be among the first to subscribe to this last assertion. Our very notion of causality, according to *The Philosophy of Physics* of Max Planck,

"cannot be demonstrated any more than it can be logically refuted: it is neither correct nor incorrect; it is a heuristic principle; it points the way, and . . . it is the most valuable pointer that we possess in order to find a path through the confusion of events, and in order to know in what direction the scientific investigation must proceed so that it shall reach useful results. The law of causality lays hold of the awakening soul of the child and compels it continually to ask why; it accompanies the scientist through the whole course of his life and continually places new problems before him."[1]

Thus is human truth made in the likeness of its axioms and methods. To the scientist, truth is that which everyone has been given a chance to discuss and no one can discuss any longer for the time being. It is a battle which ends temporarily like that of Corneille's hero fighting against the Moors, because there is no warrior left on the battlefield, and there are as yet no reinforcements within sight—until the next "last war."

The scientist is anti-doctrinal by nature. Even a biologist like Claude Bernard, who lived during the golden age of positivism, rejected positivism, as he would "avoid every species of system, because systems are not found in nature, but only in the mind of man. Positivism, like the philosophic systems which it rejects in the name of science, has the fault of being a system." And so, to Claude Bernard, experimental medicine, far from being a new system, was, on the contrary, the negation of all systems. Its advent would then "cause all individual views to disappear from the science, to be replaced by impersonal and general theories which, as in other sciences, would be only a regular and

[1] Max Planck, *The Philosophy of Physics,* translated by W. H. Johnston, New York: W. W. Norton Company, 1936, pp. 82, 83.

logical co-ordination of facts furnished by science." [2]

It is only natural, then, that neither the mathematician nor the natural scientist will have anything to do with human authority. When he carried on his research on the problem of the vacuum, Pascal thus came to grips with a Jesuit who proceeded on the authority of Aristotle. Let me advise you to read some day the *Fragment of a Preface to the Treatise on the Vacuum,* which is soon to appear in translation in the *Great Shorter Works of Pascal.*[3]

Proper Jurisdiction Restored

In this all-important document the great Christian scholar lays down as a primary principle that it is absolutely necessary to restore to experimental science the naturalistic and rationalistic method which properly belongs to it. He therefore pities "the blindness of those who offer only authority as their proof in matters of physics, instead of setting forth proofs based on reasoning or experimentation." We must give heart, he says, "to those timid people who dare not invent anything in physics." Now we know who some of those timid fellows were.

Father Noël was one of them; in fact, he stood out as Pascal's unhappy opponent. In a previous letter

[2] Claude Bernard, *Introduction à la Médecine Expérimentale,* translated by Henry C. Greene, Ann Arbor: Edwards Bros., 1940, pp. 221, 218.

[3] By The Westminster Press, Philadelphia. The following translations are taken from the manuscript.

Pascal had already reminded him of "a universal rule which provides a basis for the manner in which science is treated in the schools and which is employed by people who seek what is genuinely sound and satisfies an exacting mind." We should never pass a decisive judgment either against or in favor of a proposition without affirming or denying one of the following two conditions. Either, of itself the proposition seems so clearly and so distinctly evident to the senses or to reason, as the case may be, that the mind has no grounds for doubting its certainty; this is what we call *principles* or *axioms,* such as, for example, *if equals are added to equals, the sums will be equal.* Or it is deduced by infallible and necessary conclusions from such principles or axioms on whose certainty depends the full certainty of the conclusions which were carefully drawn therefrom. An example of this kind is that *the three angles of a triangle are equal to two right angles.* Everything based on one of these two conditions is certain and authentic, and all that is based on neither of them passes for doubtful and uncertain. "Apart from such scientific rigor," added Pascal, "we can only speak now of *vision,* now of *caprice,* at times of *fancy,* sometimes of *idea,* and at most of *fine thought.*"

That is that. Now let us mark the reservation which follows immediately on the preceding statements. "And we reserve for the mysteries of faith, which the

Holy Spirit himself has revealed, this submission of spirit which directs our belief to mysteries that are hidden from the senses and from reason."

But, then, what were some of the novelty-seeking theologians of those days doing with such mysteries? Let us revert to the *Fragment of a Preface to the Treaty on the Vacuum* for our answer. It seems that the very same people—meaning here Jesuits like Father Noël —who would offer authority alone as their proof in matters where only reasoning and experimentation are called for, resort solely to reasoning in theology instead of to the authority of the Scriptures and the Church Fathers. To Pascal, then, they seem foolhardy people whose insolence should be confounded.

Thus Pascal drew a sharp dividing line between scientific matter pertaining to rationalism and naturalism on the one hand, and, on the other, the mysteries of faith which are God's, and pertain to theology.

As we take that position three centuries after Pascal it must be with the frank admission that a part of what Pascal classified under the heading of theology has now been claimed by new disciplines. Nevertheless, the basic principle formulated by him is left intact.

The Method Put To The Test

To all intent and purpose, the mathematical sciences are not affected by this most vital of all issues. Neither

are the sciences of nature affected, apart from the fact
that the data of revelation, according to which this is
a created and God-controlled universe, enrich considerably the notion of cosmos which we owe to the
Greeks. There is no conflict thus far, as every element
of our problem slips nicely into position.

As we come to the social sciences, especially history,
the advantage is decidedly on the side of the Christian
scholar. He at least will be protected from the modern
secularized views wherein the notions of Progress and
Evolution have been so strangely merged. Document-
ing a work recently published in the series of the
American Philosophical Society, I had to canvass the
background of this question. Great was my amaze-
ment to realize how artificial the process of merging
had been. We will clarify this sufficiently by noting
that the evolution element appears once more in this
case to have been arbitrarily lifted from the biological
realm where it belonged, and applied, in turn, in the
most hit-and-miss way, to data where it never did nor
ever will belong. As for the element of Progress, it
seems that, as a distant cousin of long-since forgotten
Christian ancestors, it became a stepchild of Enlightenment and is now totally estranged in our post-war
world.

This is not a side issue in this series of lectures. We
know, do we not?—that writers in our day force the
contents of the Bible into such categories of "Evolu-

tion-Progress" foreign to its central message. Some of the subject matter in the Book of books becomes material for anthropological speculation. As these authors proceed from the crudeness of lowly origins to the refinement of highly idealistic notions of religion, are they not rewriting the Bible in a rather daring manner? For with them sin becomes an evolutionary survival from man's animal origins—which view, by the way, proves to be quite unfair to animals! Contemporary "primitives" so-called, some of whom turned out to have been degenerate,[4] are most gratuitously made to represent, somehow, the pattern for our distant ancestors. Yet considering the brain size of the Neanderthal type, for example, and what we know of his life for good measure, it seems that those of our distant ancestors who can be traced back with any certainty were as intelligent as we are. Their main trouble, doubtless, was that they lacked labor-saving devices, and therefore could not devise accelerated programs!

To proceed, Bible material is more or less arranged according to the now familiar pattern of "Evolution-Progress." The God of the Old Testament is said to have been first "conceived of" as an awe-inspiring divinity, finally to become in modern man's enlightened understanding an "Invisible Friend" no longer

---

[4] See for example Raoul Allier, *Le Non-Civilisé et Nous,* Paris: Payot, 1927, especially Chap. III "Magie et désintégration morale," pp. 86-131.

to be feared. The fact is, fear as well as love enters, even in our day, into the notion of that which is called "sacred." While it is true that we have in the Bible a progressive revelation culminating in the incarnation of the Son of God, nevertheless, God remains, even and especially in the teaching of Jesus, the awe-inspiring Sovereign to be feared. How would it be, may I ask, if someone properly selecting, classifying, and organizing his material, wrote a paradoxical history of the evolution of the "idea" of God from Abraham, the friend of God, to the Jonathan Edwards of "Sinners in the Hands of an Angry God"? Far from being facetious in these last remarks, I am only availing myself of a use of irony which is perfectly valid, according to Scripture. Pascal has a great page on the subject.

The Method Further Clarified

As we proceed from the social sciences through ethico-religious realities, we feel the need for further clarification of the distinction between what pertains to rationalism and naturalism on the one hand, and, on the other, what proves to be an authoritative matter of revelation.

Let us find our example in the case of one of the most respected scholars in our day, Professor A. T. Olmstead, Professor of Oriental History at the University of Chicago. In his recent book, *Jesus in the Light of History*, he seeks reasons for the failure of Jesus to marry, soon admitting his strange quest to be "quite futile." Why, then, raise such a shocking question, some of you will ask? But this is not the point at issue. What is interesting is the mental attitude of Professor Olmstead as he faces his problem. Jesus' failure to marry, he writes, "cannot be explained as due to consciousness of a future mission, for this consciousness did not come to Jesus until decades after He had reached the normal age of marriage." [5] Now, how can any historian know when you or I became aware of such or such a notion? How may we know ourselves, even?

This I give as a typical instance of the unreality and irrelevance of what is called objective historiography. We have come far beyond the "peril of modernizing Jesus," as you will well realize without my having to call the thing by name. Let us rather see here a decidedly misplaced use of objectivity. Such objectivity would, indeed, seem to belong to the realm of geometry, for, as Pascal wrote, the characteristic trait of the geometrician who is only a geometrician is that he does not see what is in front of him! Need we add that such apparent lack of discretion would seem to disqualify the purely secular historical method in the realm of Christian scholarship? Jesus is neither a curve nor a diagram. There comes a moment when

[5] A. T. Olmstead, *Jesus in the Light of History*, New York: Scribner's, 1942. p. 56.

would-be accuracy becomes so inadequate as to miss the point.

Now, secular scholarship may try to amend its methods by using more imagination, and this has been attempted—only too much. Concluding an agnostic study of "the Problem of Jesus," Professor Charles Guignebert of the Sorbonne had to denounce the abuse of constantly gratuitous hypotheses—*"abus de l'hypothèse en l'air"* [6] is his untranslatable French way of putting it. Yet the learned book of Professor Guignebert misses the point also. Like Matthew Arnold, he does not seem to have been on speaking terms with the Divinity.

Kierkegaard would help us throw light on such misunderstandings, as he draws a dividing line which practically coincides with that of Pascal, followed thus far. The great Danish philosopher distinguishes between scientific matter, which naturally becomes an object of acquisition to which the personal life of the teacher is accidental, and ethico-religious matter, realities wherein commitment is the essential thing. "What nonsense it is therefore that instead of following Christ or the Apostles and suffering as they suffered, one should become professor—of what?" Of the fact that Christ was crucified or that the Apostles were scourged?

[6] Charles Guignebert, *Le Problème de Jésus*, Paris: Flammarion, 1914, p. 157.

Kierkegaard remarks that "the Professor" was a later invention indeed, "for it was about the time when Christianity began to go backward, and the culminating point of 'the professor's' ascent coincides exactly with our age, when Christianity is entirely abolished." [7] We recognize here a variation on the Kierkegaardian theme: "The Christianity of the New Testament no longer exists." This painful outcry voices an identical protest, in Kierkegaard as in Pascal, a protest rooted in a similar evangelical consciousness.

But there is still more bitterness in the ironical protest of Kierkegaard than in Pascal's earnest memoir on *Comparaison des Chrétiens des Premiers Temps avec Ceux d'Aujourd'hui*. The Danish Pascal wittily imagines that

"Judas Iscariot was not, as indeed in reality he was, a man in despair who in an instant of fury sells his master for the paltry thirty pieces of silver—where in the smallness of the sum there is a kind of extenuation, as also after a sort in his frightful end. No, Judas is a much more highly cultured man, calm, and in possession of a shrewder understanding of life, of profit. So he goes to the high priests and says to them: 'I am willing to betray him. But now hear my conditions. I don't care much about getting a large sum once for all which I might squander in a few years. No, I wish something certain yearly. I am a young man, well and strong, having in all human probability the prospect

[7] Walter Lowrie, *A Short Life of Kierkegaard*, Princeton University Press, 1942, pp. 228, 230.

of a long life before me—and I could wish to lead (married and with a family) an agreeable life with rich opportunity for enjoyment. That is the price.' This, according to my notion, is a whole quality more odious—nor do I believe that anything so odious could have occurred in the earlier times, it is reserved for our intelligent times. It is easily seen that I have represented Judas a little *à la* professor." [8]

Severe words, these. As is the case with every parable, they should not be pressed too far. Certainly they should not be made to affirm that Christian scholarship did not count in the consideration of Kierkegaard. His whole life-work would rise up as a protest against this. These words, then, attest to the fact of Christianity [9] as it finally emerges from the consideration of the reverent historian. Surely the time has come when we should set forth and act on it.

Rather are these words meant to reveal to us the great divide which all along we have been trying to detect—one which further separates in the midst of ethico-religious realities modern values from Christian virtues, the proud mind from the reverent mind, and Greek intellectualism from the Hebrew-Christian way of thinking—the latter proving to be, in the last analysis, *existential*. Kierkegaard's words must be read

[8] *Ibid.*, pp. 230, 231.
[9] Cf. P. Carnegie Simpson, *The Fact of Christ*, New York, London and Edinburgh: Fleming H. Revell Company, 1901.

in the context of his experience. He finally parted ways with Hegel in order to find the truth, which was truth for himself, and to appropriate that discovery. This meant turning away from pure speculation, from the System, and directing his efforts to reality, so as to exist, to stand out—*ex-stare*. Heidegger suggests the same experience as the fact of *Da-sein, In-der-Welt-sein*—which Walter Lowrie translated "thereness," (the fact to be in the world).

First of all, there must be a deliberate renunciation of the purely esthetic enjoyment of life; then, a lone venturing forth far upon the deep, with seventy thousand fathoms of water under us, in the firm assurance that one shall be supported, then be met, in the fulness of time, to be given at last sealed orders. As in the case of Isaac, this venture of faith may imply a temporary, awe-inspiring suspension of the "ethical" until one be found by the Truth.

Now, tell me, once this has happened, how could the Lord's free man, without great betrayal to himself and to his Master, make Truth the object of a detached, pleasure-seeking occupation?

On his deathbed Kierkegaard said to his old friend, Pastor Boesen, "You must note that I have seen from the very inside of Christianity." [10] So also will the Christian student consider from the inside phenomena which are observed from the outside by purely pro-

[10] Walter Lowrie, *A Short Life of Kierkegaard, op. cit.,* p. 239.

fessional men. This may be one of the reasons why these two classes of men will not get the same viewpoint.

To the new focus suggested by Pascal and Kierkegaard we now turn.

CHAPTER V

Toward a Biblical Perspective

BIBLICAL CATEGORIES

AFTER THE DILEMMA of Christian scholarship has been settled in the realm of methodology, we find ourselves wiser, I hope, facing the treatment of subject matter. The question, you will remember, was no longer how to formulate the Christian faith so as not to create problems for Greek thought, but how to proceed from a Greek mysticism, which must not be confused with Christianity, back to the true Messianic categories fulfilled in Jesus Christ.

Precisely because the problem had been formulated in the first of these two ways, it seemed to demand that the Gospel and the First Epistle of John be stressed as the proper restatement in Greek categories of an unbearably Jewish hope and faith.

The term *Logos* confronts us right at the beginning of the Fourth Gospel, and it belongs to Greek philosophy since the day of Heraclitus. Does this imply that the deeper meaning of this same Gospel is to be looked for in Hellenistic cosmic interpretations, in the transformations of Plato's Demiurge, and especially in the conciliation by Philo of Alexandria, of Plato and Isaiah? That the Fourth Gospel is so different in character from the Synoptic Gospels, that it is basically foreign to the data of Jewish Christianity? That we have here on the whole a case of Greek mysticism as opposed to the eschatalogy of the Synoptic Gospels? Does it mean that, because John reports warnings of Jesus against "another" coming in His name, he is referring to a certain rebellion put down by Hadrian in the years 132 to 135? That therefore John is such a late Gospel that it belongs essentially to our Western ways of looking at the Divinity?

Were this the case, many a Christian would renounce on the spot the Fourth Gospel, and by the same token perhaps would consider renouncing the Christian revelation altogether, as indeed many did within the last generation. Yet by now these unfortunate ones have been proved wrong. An "Unknown Gospel" has come to the fore, whose fragments were gathered and edited from papyri by H. Idris Bell and T. C. Skeat; and, furthermore, a portion of that same Fourth Gospel was deposited in the John Rylands Library and in 1935 was edited by C. H. Roberts. The fact is now firmly established that our Fourth Gospel must have been known in Egypt somewhere around A. D. 100, and must be placed together with the First Epistle of John somewhere between the years of our Lord 90 and 100. By the same token, the Fourth

Gospel could not then conceivably refer to a revolt put down over some forty years later. Furthermore, a closer examination of the same brings to light strong eschatological elements, while Philo's doctrine on the function of the *Logos* appears to a great degree, as "a substitute for Messianic hopes." [1]

As to the pre-existence of the Christ, which has been associated with the *Logos* in the first verse of John's Gospel, that is also clearly stated or implied in the earliest Gospel, the one according to Mark (about A. D. 65); also in the Letters of Paul to the Philippians (about A. D. 59-61), to the Romans (A. D. 56-57), and to the Galatians (A. D. 52-58). As a matter of fact, a backward glance along this chronological line to the more primitive tradition, proves more and more to us the unqualified humanity of Jesus. In like manner the grandeur of the *Logos* revelation is more sharply focused, especially as stated in the Letter of Paul to the Philippians (2:5-7): "Christ Jesus, who, though he was in the form of God, did not count equality with God a thing to be grasped, but emptied himself, taking the form of a servant, being born in the likeness of men."

It is true that, as we start from that earlier tradition and progress toward John's Gospel, Jesus' "emptying of Self" appears less evident. The mighty works of

[1] Marvin R. Vincent, *Word Studies in the New Testament*, New York: Charles Scribner's Sons, 1889, v. 2, 31.

the Lord become rather more numerous and more wonderful, until we are brought face to face with the glorious, the divine Self-Disclosure. In certain quarters, this is interpreted as a tendency to make God of a mere man. But, then, an assertion like that does not make sense, since all our writers are in agreement on the pre-existence of Jesus. In fact, it would lead to absurdities when applied in other realms to more primitive traditions. For instance, Jesus is presented more emphatically as a teacher in Luke than in Mark. Would that mean that the teaching element has been progressively added, and imply that there was an early stage in the pre-literary tradition when there was no teaching at all? We know better than that.

The fact is, while Luke took over about one-half of Mark, he has, in common with Matthew, over two hundred verses, found in a primitive written source, which scholars call *Quelle,* the German word for "source." Abbreviated as "Q," that particular source has not survived, but in so far as a restoration of it can be made, it was essentially an early record of the sayings of Jesus, perhaps in the form of a manual of conduct for converts.

And so the sayings of Jesus were present in the earliest tradition. We have no reason to doubt that the same might not hold true in the case of the mighty works of Jesus. As scholars have now come to look at it, the Gospel appears from a critical viewpoint to have been a presentation at once of authoritative wisdom-sayings of Jesus and of the record of the Living God's mighty intervention in the web of history.

Yet this is the way the problem which we stated above appears to a contemporary mind, reverent but critical: "When the historian attempts to go back of the faith of the Early Church, he immediately runs into insuperable difficulties. He cannot lay his finger on a cause even approximately adequate to the effect. Was it the resurrection of Jesus? But what can such an answer mean to the hisorian? And yet what answer which seems at all adequate *can* be expressed in the terms of 'scientific' history?" There is always a gap between what the Gospel tells us about Jesus "and what subsequent events tell us He was. And somewhere in that gap—unrecovered and unrecoverable—lies the secret of the mighty impact which Jesus of Nazareth made upon His age." [2]

On *this* side of the gap detected in the above quotation are to be found, as contemporary scholars are careful to bring out, Greek influences early at work in Hellenistic Judaism, such as would clothe the Incarnation of the *Logos* in attributes of Wisdom originally ascribed to Orphic hope. And mystical philosophy did the same thing. Hence a new Christian version of current pagan myths was disclosed, and eventually recog-

[2] John Knox, *The Man Christ Jesus,* Chicago, New York: Willett, Clark & Co., 1941, p. 68.

nized as being superior to them because it grew out of history and *ipso facto* became part of the warp and woof, the intricate texture, of a great saga of salvation.

To say even that much, however, is to reintegrate into the equation the God of Israel fulfilling in and through history His redeeming purpose. Thus a jolt is felt as we pass into a new climate. We feel it even in the midst of an Hellenistic Judaism reading the Old Testament in Greek and becoming familiar with such identifications as that of Moses with Osiris, Orpheus, or Hermes. And a gap is still gaping wide somewhere between the days of our Lord and this strange new world.

We might even locate this gap. It is laid bare by the "disgraceful" Passion narratives which were in all probability the first New Testament documents to be written down. They, at least, have no parallels in pagan myths. As Higher Criticism invites us to approach our Bible in much the same way wherewith geologists view the strata of the earth, we may temporarily borrow the language of geology to say that we discover at this point *a fault*. Doubtless this fault was created after Jesus had yielded up the spirit "and the earth shook, and the rocks were split," in the words of the Matthew narrative.

Such is the ugly gap which only the Resurrection can bridge. And this, to our mind, explains the insistence Paul placed on the fact that "if Christ had not been raised, then our preaching is in vain and your faith is in vain" (1 Cor. 15:14). The process through which the Gospel was to conquer the Greek world was not one of adaptation by means of syncretistic accretions. Neither was it an instance of narrow Jewish national and political opinion forced into the Greek mold. Rather was the new wine, harvested in spite of the wicked husbandmen, poured into wine skins made on the old prophetic pattern. Let it be proclaimed far and wide that the Lord remains Owner of His Vineyard, and that His Purpose must be carried out.

A. G. Hebert, whom we are following at this point,[3] makes it clear in his reference to Bible categories that the Temple had been allowed to fall and be destroyed only to be raised up again, so that the Call of the Gentiles might be realized on a universal plane. What had been impossible to men was now made possible by the Living God. A Biblical universalism emerged, which was in line with the eternal Purpose of the great Doer of redeeming things. Greeks as well as Jews were to be gathered in, on His own terms, from the streets, the lanes, the highways and hedges, that His House might be filled. Neither in the Mountain of the Lord nor in Jerusalem were they to lift up their hearts in worship that excluded all others, but, in-

[3] A. G. Hebert, *The Throne of David*, London: Faber & Faber, 1941.

stead, the people were being brought together into the Jerusalem which is above as an Elect Race, a Royal Priesthood, a Holy Nation, a People for God's own Purpose all over the world. Thus, in the Risen Messiah's own Creation, members of the believing Remnant included many Gentiles, and became the true Israel. As for the Jews who had rejected the Corner Stone now erected in its proper place, they were, in consequence, found wanting and lost their own claims to inheritance. Paul, in his Letter to the Romans, devotes many words to the new status of these Jews (Chapters 9-11).

The road to final conquest of the Greek world was not, then, a way of appeasement along which Hebrew-Christian notions were made to lose their distinctive color and shape, as the salt of the earth its savor. On the contrary, we today, living in a time of crisis, seeing a new ecumenism among the Parliaments of Religion in vain search for methods whereby the Church of Christ might make her voice heard and her message effective—we should realize clearly what such theological rehabilitation means. It should mean, first of all,

"that Gentile Christians enter on the inheritance of Israel. They learn to look on the sacred history of the Old Testament as their own, treating Abraham, Isaac and Jacob as their own forefathers—and to such an extent has this taken place that in the case of many nations, including our own, the old pagan national mythologies have dropped out of the popular mind, and the Old Testament has stepped into their place. They use the Old Testament as the Book of the Church of which they are members, they treat Abraham, Isaac, and Jacob as their own forefathers. . . . Above all, the Gentile Christians pray in the language of the Old Testament. The Psalter is the standard book of the Church's prayer and praise, and her whole liturgical thought is built on a spiritual interpretation of the Old Testament.

"Here we have the true fulfilment of the Old Testament prophecies which tell of the Gentiles coming to Zion. We find in New Testament times what we do not find in Old Testament times: missionaries going out to proclaim the Gospel. They can do so now without infringing on the Biblical principle of the gathering-together of mankind to a Center. The worship of God through the Messiah, in Spirit and in Truth, is not localized at the geographical Jerusalem; it can happen now in every place where the *ecclesia,* Israel, is." [4]

This is the Delectable Country through which we may travel, once the luminous span has been fully restored, allowing us to walk back and forth.

CHRIST, THE MEASURE

The "luminous span" of which I speak is, of course, the Resurrection, an act of God who "was in Christ reconciling the world to himself" (2 Cor. 5:19).

[4] *Ibid.,* pp. 231, 232.

In the glorification of the Messiah of the true Israel, we have "the first fruits of those who have fallen asleep." Yet we can think on such ineffable realities only while basing our reasoning on the ultimate foundation of analogy. Such an analogy presupposes faith in the mighty God of Israel as a third term of comparison. For it is only when such a term is introduced in our equations that we are enabled to transcend our human contradictions. Erich Frank pertinently remarked in a note appended to his Flexner Lectures [5] that the fundamental importance of the principle of analogy has been sadly neglected in modern philosophy. Yet it had never been questioned by Aristotle himself, and his "Analogy of Being" was carefully interpreted by Thomas Aquinas and the medieval philosophers. Nay, even Plato emphasized it. The author of *The Republic* knew that since no final knowledge is attainable wherewith to describe the fate of the soul after death, a poetical imagery had to be used to suggest it. His own poetical imagery of the other life we do not accept, of course, whether it be found in *The Republic,* or in other dialogues, such as *Gorgias, Phædo,* or *Phædrus.* What we are interested in is the vindication by the most outstanding Greek and medieval philosophers of the validity, nay, of the *necessity* of the ultimate principle of analogy, which undergirds at

[5] Erich Frank, *Philosophical Understanding and Religious Truth,* Oxford University Press, 1945, n. 63, p. 181.

every point the Paulinian suggestive distinction between the 'written code' which kills, and the Spirit
which gives life. (2 Cor. 3:6).

While the end of those who live as enemies of the
Cross of Christ is destruction (Phil. 3:18, 19) those who
are in Christ know Him and the Power of His resurrection (Phil. 3:10). Their name has now been placed
in the Book of Life. Such is the vivid imagery wherein
the New Testament suggests the status of those who,
even now, *have* eternal life. This status implies at the
same time present enjoyment and future consummation. The surrendered soul is in the hands of the
Living God and therefore needs fear no longer. Yet
such status is necessarily expressed in the language
of man, which comes short of its glory. To press its
literalism into contradictory terms on the human level
is to ignore the ineffable character of the Divine
Reality with which it is dealing. Let us therefore, in
this new awareness, read afresh Paul's statement to
the Corinthians:

"What is sown is perishable, what is raised is imperishable. It is sown in dishonor, it is raised in glory. It is sown
in weakness, it is raised in power. It is sown a physical
body, it is raised a spiritual body. I tell you this, brethren:
flesh and blood cannot inherit the imperishable. . . . For
this perishable nature must *put on* the imperishable, and
this mortal nature must *put on* immortality. When the
perishable puts on immortality, then shall come to pass the

saying that is written: Death is swallowed up in victory. O death, where is thy victory? O death, where is thy sting? The sting of death is sin, and the power of sin is the law. But thanks be to God, who gives us victory through our Lord Jesus Christ. Therefore, my beloved brethren, be steadfast, immovable, always abounding in the work of the Lord, knowing that in the Lord your labor is not in vain."

That *is* a Gospel. With it we pass—*ex umbris et imaginibus in veritatem*—out of shadows and images into the truth. It secures the 'access to God' foreshadowed in the Old Testament and fulfilled in Christ, whereby we may enjoy the true Sabbath, that is, the rest provided for the people of God, which is spoken of in The Letter to the Hebrews. Here we have not a set of laws and observances as understood by the Pharisees, not the abstention of thirty-nine classes of actions and other such prohibitive rules, but a peace and joy in the present as a foretaste of the future consummation of glory. For Christ is the Measure of the Sabbath, as He is the Measure and ideal Pattern of Bible categories.

Just as the Gospel and First Letter of John were used to aid in the evangelization of the Greeks—even at the cost of wrong interpretations sometimes, may not The Letter to the Hebrews be now used to revitalize Greek mysticism? It was written at a time of crisis to arouse the Christians of Rome from indifference to the genuine character and peculiar worth of their faith. These features are brought out in the best Greek language of the whole New Testament by means of a point-by-point reference to the Old Testament. The author shows how the Christian faith interprets as it fulfils. A scriptural use of analogy guardedly paves the way to the New Jerusalem in heaven, for a Platonism familiar with the distinction of the two worlds, the phenomenal and the real. In a manner true to the Biblical pattern, the Letter implies that the Gentiles are still coming on their way to Zion. Only they are doing it more easily now that the Kingdom of God has come in their midst. There is no mistake possible in realizing who is Lord, the Christ or Cæsar.

We are now coming closer to "what is truth for us," as Kierkegaard would say. It is noteworthy that in his Gospel John uses the Hebrew phrase "to do the truth" (3:21). "He who does what is true comes to the light, that it may be clearly seen that his deeds have been wrought of God." The phrase "comes to the light" is itself suggestive of the now familiar Old Testament pattern, according to which the Gentiles advance toward Zion.

It would seem that one of the reasons why our Lord chose His disciples among fishermen and other such common folk is that these were not likely to misinterpret His words in terms of a purely theoretical mode of existence. Here we may have the key also, or one of the keys, to the election of Israel by the Living God. The truth *is* life, and as such can best be disclosed through the history of a divinely disciplined people whose notions are, first and foremost, notions of flesh and blood.

It becomes evident, then, that He who *is* "the way, the truth, and the life" is the one Guide to the Book, for its categories and patterns find in Him their true meaning and expression. And He is their fulfilment. In Him is Christianity summed up.

The Testimony of the Earliest Documents

As we now come, with a personal concern, to the earliest documents regarding the Christ, it must be in the awareness that even the most accurate contemporaneous sources would provide poor help in a real understanding of our Lord for him who did not love the Lord and did not await salvation through Him. It must also be remembered that only after the Holy Spirit, or Counselor, had been given to them were the disciples themselves guided unto truth.

To all intents and purposes, the earliest Christian documents that research can get at, or that scholarship will take on, are found to be either a proclamation of the good news for non-Christians, or an exhortation designed for those who were already Christians. It is either *kerygma* or *didache*. Now, what the New Testament calls *kerygma* is actually the message of salvation. The word is derived from *keryssein,* a verb occurring sixty-one times in the New Testament. Archibald M. Hunter, Yates Professor of New Testament Greek and Exegesis at Mansfield College, Oxford, draws our attention to the fact that it is the verb which Jesus used to describe His mission (Mark 1:38; Luke 4:18 ff.); the verb also which describes the work of his twelve "envoys" (Mark 6:12); again, the verb which describes the function of the earliest Christian missionaries (Romans 10:14). Professor Hunter further reminds us that while this verb is normally rendered "preach," yet the associations which have gathered around our word "preaching" may easily mislead us at this point, for the Greek verb does not imply an edifying exhortation delivered in a melodious tone; it means the *proclamation* of an event, *i.e.,* the coming of God's redemptive Rule in Jesus Christ.[6] And to this day, the gist of all true preaching will be such a proclamation. As for the *Didache,* it is concerned with exhortation designed for those who were already Christians. A fine example of such moral and spiritual instruction is to be found in Paul's First Letter to the Corinthians.

In both cases scholars are brought by the earliest documents face to face with the testimony of the Early Church to the Christ. Indeed, the earliest mes-

---

[6] Archibald M. Hunter, *The Message of the New Testament,* Philadelphia: The Westminster Press, 1944, p. 24.

sage of the Church, the burden of the Good News,
or Gospel, was not, "Follow this beautiful Master
and do the best you can," but, "The Risen Lord." As
stated above, the first documents to be written down
were in all probability the Passion narratives.

THE ORIGINAL CREEDAL FORM

It is not enough, therefore, to speak of the original
Christian faith as being Christ-*centered*. It was Jesus
Christ Himself, who came *into* our history to be our
Lord, our Light, our very Life; Jesus Christ who was
put in a category by Himself, in the realm of things
divine. The one essential primitive formulation of the
Good News was the simple statement: "Jesus is Lord,"
—nay, the very name Jesus Christ constituted the most
compressed creed. The earliest confession of faith
might very well have been the watchword of the Ara-
maic-speaking Mother Church in Jerusalem, the *Mara-
natha* of 1 Corinthian 16:22. This, "Our *Lord,* come!",
you will recall, appears at the end of the Epistle as
a salutation in Paul's own hand, and is opposed to
anyone who "has no love for the Lord." So it is at
the same time a curse and a prayer—one of the short-
est, as well as one of the earliest, prayers of the Christian faith. And by their prayer ye shall know their
faith!

Now, as we all remember, the full humanity of
Jesus must be asserted side by side with the original

creedal form "Jesus is Lord." We need to be reminded again and again of the Lord's real manhood, for the tendency during the early centuries of the Christian era was to stress the Lord's deity to a point where His manhood was denied. Our contemporary mysticism, on the other hand, has led us so far in the opposite direction that we need to be reminded of that other extremist position held by Gnostics, Docetists, and Appolinarians. Such a tendency was indeed encouraged by the philosophers of their day, the more so because most of them were anxious to deal with problems raised by the new faith as to the true nature of the Christ.

These observations lead us, incidentally, to the strange discovery that extremes meet at this very point. For Alexandria, with her Greek background, began her thinking about God in heaven, so to speak. Thus she found difficulty in the humanity of Christ. Modern mysticism also thinks of God in heaven, but having, in due process of time, made of Jesus a mere man, its problem is now to formulate the religious life of Jesus in terms acceptable to nature and to reason. Let us see in the above statement one more striking illustration of the thoroughness with which a Hebrew-Christian faith has been adapted to an essentially Greek civilization, once adopted by that civilization.

Meanwhile, as scholars carry on their wearying search for the "historical" Jesus through the Gospels and Epistles, through early collections of the sayings of Jesus, and notes on His life possibly written in Aramaic, still this much remains true: the "Gospel before the Gospels" remains the Gospel. And in this Gospel countless early believers testify to the Lordship of the One, clearly pictured from one end of the New Testament to the other, and responsible for its unity. Although oversimplification gets in the way of anyone seeking to blaze a trail in the midst of extremely complex source-material, the essential point is well brought out by Professor William Manson in his Cunningham Lectures [7] as he remarks that in the sphere of our Lord's spirit, all Messianic conceptions have been absorbed.

THE CHRIST IN A CLASS BY HIMSELF

Whether we speak in terms of a Life, of a Power, of a Kingdom, or simply of a religion, Christianity, in the end, can be defined only as Jesus Christ Himself. Again, the main thesis of Christology, the supreme affirmation of the early Christians, is that the Christ belongs to the category of the divine. No longer can we separate the Messianic reign of God from God's own revelation in the One through whom He reconciles the world unto Himself.

The propagating power and conquering force of

[7] William Manson, *Jesus the Messiah*, Philadelphia: The Westminster Press, 1946, p. 215.

this faith have left on the records of the first two centuries an imprint that is unmistakable. In his magnificent book on *The Apostolic Preaching and Its Developments*,[8] Professor C. H. Dodd of Cambridge has clearly shown that there was no deviation from the original content of the Gospel as found in 1 Corinthians 15:1-11. Praying to her unique, absolute, final and cosmic Lord, who could say: "Before Abraham was, I am," the Early Church was truly a remnant. According to Gibbon, this remnant made the record that it did because it remained separate, exclusive; it refused to compromise. To the extent that conflict, nay, death were willingly undergone so that Christianity might displace other religions, men were won to the living Lord through the living Lord. This dynamic faith was quick to generate and sustain Christianity in the mission field at a time when there was not in evidence the grave question of "re-thinking missions." It is such genuine faith which fills churches down to our day.

Remembering that logic will always accomplish far less than love, the Christian preacher joyfully acknowledges the truth in non-Christian religions. He knows that only such truth as is in them, has enabled them to survive and has given them whatever power they enjoy. But he never fails to make it clear in the

[8] C. H. Dodd, *The Apostolic Preaching and Its Developments*, Chicago: Willett, Clark & Co., 1937.

next breath that there is no truth or good in them which is not found in purer and fuller form in Christianity. In the words of Robert E. Speer, the non-Christian religions "are expressions of the religious nature of man. Whatever good and truth they possess is inadequate. They provide no way of salvation or of deliverance from sin. They are deficient in their ethical and social ideals and dynamic. They have no adequate idea of God and no Atoning and Living Saviour. Dark evils and untruths have found shelter in them. They express but also encumber the religious nature of man." [9]

You will grant me that these are not private opinions. As Alfred E. Smith would have put it, I am merely looking at the record. I have been stating facts all along. Admittedly, such sayings as are found in this Apostolic preaching would be hard sayings for any naturalistically minded person to listen to very long. Even the early disciples found them to be so as their discipleship was being tested by doctrine: "This is a hard saying, who can listen to it?" they once said to Jesus. And we are told that from that time on many of them walked no more with the Master and went their way. Then as this same Master asked the twelve whether they also would go away, Simon Peter answered, "Lord, to whom shall we go? You

[9] Robert E. Speer, *The Finality of Jesus Christ*, New York, London: Fleming H. Revell Co., 1933, p. 334.

have the words of eternal life," whereupon followed the ultimate confession: "We have believed, and have come to know, that you are the Holy One of God." (John 6:60-69). Again, we are told that Peter's confession of the Messianic character of his Lord called forth from the Christ the striking statement: "Flesh and blood has not revealed this to you, but my Father who is in heaven" (Matthew 16:16, 17). A capital distinction, that, and from the very lips of the Christ, between the naturalistic and the Biblical points of view in matters of Christian faith and doctrine.

THE FINALITY OF THE CHRIST

The Christ did not come to found one more religion better than the others and comparable to them. He came *into* history as the Self-Revelation of the Father. He is all we know of God. Besides, as according to Scripture the main function of the Spirit of God is to bear witness of the Christ with our spirit, the Son is truly the God of men.

Walter M. Horton may well call Him in a happy title *Our Eternal Contemporary,* and comment on the difficulty of distinguishing between the Living Christ and the Holy Spirit. "The Holy Spirit," he states, "was felt by the Early Church to be both the abiding presence of the Risen Lord, and the abiding presence of that divine power which had raised him from the dead. God sent Jesus, Jesus sent the Spirit, God sent the Spirit. . . . The Spirit, or the Living Christ, is the most *immediate* and *inward* form in which we experience God." [10] Based upon such sound doctrine, a regenerated mysticism may lead to a richer life. When, on the other hand, the Biblical categories have been abandoned, a shapeless mysticism will offer only a weak line of retreat. This will be confirmed by strong Christians such as George Müller, whose life of prayer at times had been parched, precisely whenever his thoughts were too long drawn away from the Bible.

In the opinion of Robert E. Speer, one must insist on what he calls, in the title of his best book, *The Finality of Jesus Christ*.[11] All other masters are only human masters; they must give way to the One Lord in whom our questions are answered. It is true, therefore, that in its original and authentic form Christianity is not to be classified with other religions. Using the very direct language of Phillimore, we may say that Christianity will have nothing to do with "courtly polygamies of the soul." [12] It is incommensurable and alone, like Christ Himself, who is before all things, and in whom all things hold together (Col. 1:17).

This, then, is the Christian faith, for us as for Paul.

[10] Walter M. Horton, *Our Eternal Contemporary*, A Study of the Present-Day Significance of Jesus, New York: Harper and Brothers, 1942, p. 143.

[11] *Op. cit.*

[12] Quoted by J. Gresham Machen, *Christianity and Liberalism, op. cit.,* p. 123.

The Christian faith is a tremendous fact of cosmic import, so that it is indeed difficult to see how mere secularism could even begin to cope with it. I for one see great significance in the fact that the *Cambridge Ancient History,* the most recent synthesis and sum of our knowledge of the ancient world, refused so much as to attempt a portrait of Jesus. Some will call this a manifestation of agnosticism, and in a way they will be right. I see in it a manifestation, above all, of intellectual honesty. The plain fact of the matter is that, when scholars have done their best—or their worst—and come to the beginnings of Christianity, they find themselves inevitably confronted with this most primitive interpretation of Jesus by Peter in Acts 2:36: "God has made him both Lord and Christ, this Jesus whom you crucified." Neither should we allow ourselves to be misled by the fact of the messianic "secret" so-called, that is, by the reticence of Jesus as to His messianic character. For He knew that there was danger lest his hearers be misled by their own false, conventional idea of what the Messiah should be. They must first be initiated into the right notion of the Kingdom by His ministry in Galilee.

This teaching is in no way that of a "Messiah designate" uncertain of Himself. It is a Messianic sign in itself, the progressive revelation to men who were as yet unprepared, of a veiled mystery acknowledged only in the realm divine. In Mark, for example, we find the hearers' inquiring minds faced with the "must" of divine necessity. At the close of the Sermon on the Mount we are told that the crowds were astonished at the words of Jesus, "for he taught them as one who had authority, and not as their scribes." Jesus spoke as one who knew. As Campbell Morgan puts it, "His teaching was not a deduction from appearances, but the uttering forth of eternal principles in the speech of man"; as such it gave men "a new conception of the authority of God, as based upon the necessity of the things that are." [13] The Greeks might call "foolish" the data of such a disclosure, but this "foolishness" actually works and thus tallies with the facts as we have come to know them.

It is to be noted, moreover, that this same note of authority remains the keynote throughout the writings of the New Testament. Paul does not speculate, in the philosophical sense of the word; he always proceeds by deduction from what is taken for granted. He does not argue with his listeners and his readers; he reminds them of what is now known, and tells them to proceed on it. Those of us who seem to worry about the absence of authority in our Reformed tradition are, to all practical purposes, simply laying bare the fact that dust has too long been allowed to collect on our Bibles. Let them turn again to the New Testa-

[13] G. Campbell Morgan, *The Crises of the Christ*, New York, London & Edinburgh: Fleming H. Revell Co., 1903, 1936, p. 436.

ment and read of "the thing that has happened among us."

The French scholar Alfred Loisy, who might be called the patron of all "liberals" in our day, on finding in one of the earliest sources of the "Gospel before the Gospels" this glorious self-disclosure of Jesus: "All things are delivered unto me of my Father; and no man knoweth the Son, but the Father," commented thereon with the greatest intellectual honesty, as follows: "The Christ it designates is immortal, we may even say eternal."

One fact stands out clearly, then: if, by the expression "historical Jesus" some people have in mind a purely human figure disengaged from the "divine Christ," and as such acceptable to naturalistically minded scholars anxious to safeguard their intellectual respectability, then those people should look for it elsewhere than in the available New Testament records.

THE DUTY OF INTELLECTUAL HONESTY

The eternal question in connection with Christianity remains: What then shall we do with the Christ? To this question there may be a perfectly legitimate answer, saying in effect that He must be repudiated in view of such-and-such naturalistic presuppositions. But, then, there is also the answer of a reverent and enlightened faith. The student will sit down in front of all the documents he possesses regarding Him, and will attempt to clarify their meaning. This he will do with special attention to the differences in mental framework between the Ancients' cosmology and our own outlook. We no longer live in their three-storied cosmos, that is, on a flat earth with the revolving heavens above and the underworld beneath. Having once realized this, we can scarcely be shocked by the wording of the Apostles' Creed, for example, any more than by that of the *Commedia* of Dante.

We readily realize that if He was to be understood at all, Jesus had to speak in a language familiar to people who lived with such cosmological presuppositions. For the same reason His words were necessarily grasped and molded into mental categories and symbols involving such presuppositions. If you remember what has been said thus far as to the dividing line which sets apart the mysteries of faith from rationalistic matter pertaining to the scientific method, you will make your own Galileo's statement in *The Authority of Scripture,* "The intention of the Holy Ghost is to teach us how we shall go to Heaven, and not how the heavens go."

It is with a trembling hand, however, that we would choose to deal with the *mysterium Christi*. At the point where God breaks into our history, the wisest, as well as the safest, attitude is one of worship and reverent scholarship. We may not rewrite the New Testament

documents and fit the picture more or less into our naturalistic frame. Should we set about our inquiry with
the basic naturalistic assumption that man is the measure of all things, then, however clever, however subtle
and painstaking our labors, we might just as well have
spared ourselves the trouble. For in the end we would
merely find Lord Morley's "far-off mystic of the Galilean Hills" where had once stood the Incarnate Word.

The weakest point in David Hume's famous essay
"On Miracles" is his central statement on the impossi-
bility of the fact that a dead *man* should come to life
because that phenomenon has never been observed in
any age or country. Such reasoning reminds one of
Richard Jeffries' *Story of a Boy* in his reference to the
cruelty of the Crucifixion, to the effect that "if God
had been there, he would not have let them do it!" The
whole point is that God Himself *was* there, of course,
and according to the most primitive interpretation of
our Saviour, embedded in The Acts of the Apostles,
God had made both Lord and Christ this Jesus whom
they crucified (2:36). By losing sight of, and contact
with, the "Good News" that occurred in our midst we
should be left alone on Calvary with the dejected
philosophy of "the man under the sun." In his crudely
pessimistic language we should have to comment: That
which befalleth the sons of men befalleth beasts; as the
one dieth, so dieth the other, and a living dog is better
than a dead lion. Then would our outlook be darker

than ever, for all evidence would show that, in the words, already quoted, of James Thomson in his *City of Dreadful Night,*

> ". . . none can pierce the vast black veil uncertain
> Because there is no light beyond the curtain;
> . . . All is vanity and nothingness."

DISPELLING ILLUSIONS

Some Greek mystics will object at this point and say: "Ours is the doctrine of immortality of the soul. To us, therefore, Jesus *must* be alive even now, since all men are immortal." What they are actually saying is that Jesus must have been immortal *like everybody else.* To borrow a striking illustration from Arthur W. Hewitt, they feel that when during the same night Judas Iscariot hangs from a tree and Jesus of Nazareth on the Cross, death is the same for both. Not only have they lost sight of the uniqueness of the Christ, but, looking at death in general from this, our human level of existence, the Biblical doctrine of a life that perishes and of a Life that is everlasting has given way to a natural religion squarely based on man's belief in man. The anchor no longer holds fast to the rock; it has given way, and they are adrift.

They might as well turn frankly to the Platonic picture of Socrates playing with the hair of Phaedo, and have the chorus interpret the feeling of the play with the words: "There can no evil happen to a good man in life or death." They must be aware, however, that even this philosophy of Plato has been denounced as a rationalization of animism. John Baillie goes so far as to concede that "the reasons Plato suggests for believing in the continued existence of the soul correspond very closely to the reasons which had, from the Old Stone Age onwards, led men to believe in it." [14] This should be of special concern to these same objective scholars, as it was to William James when he came to the conclusion of his Gifford Lectures on natural religion.[15]

If Jesus be reduced to the proportions of the lay mystic, mentioned above, whose fate changed the Galilean idyll into a human tragedy, where do we stand? The Christian faith becomes the would-be faith of a candid soul who has supposedly "inherited" or "borrowed" notions which are later proven to have been erroneous, and then is said to have "developed" concepts which our present age pronounces obsolete, and to have made promises which now prove to have been made in vain. It may be smart in our day to say that Jesus "hit upon" certain ideas. Our current expression "hit or miss" spoils for me, however, all such arbitrary restoration.

What, then, is left? The fallible and often mistaken

[14] John Baillie, *And the Life Everlasting,* New York: Scribner's, 1933, p. 98.
[15] Cf. William James, *The Varieties of Religious Experience,* 1902, New York: The Modern Library, pp. 480 ff.

faith of a problematic, at best shadowy, figure, scarcely discernible through the haze of nineteen centuries, and forever questioned because of the supernatural character of early documents, so that scholars actually come to doubt His existence. Let us note in passing that the hypothesis of the "Christ myth," so-called, which caused so much excitement when popularized during the first decade of this century, is now dead for good.

The position of those who believe *with* Jesus, but not *in* Him is simply untenable. New Testament scholarship will have none of this in our day. So eminent a scholar as Professor Wilbert F. Howard, lecturer in Hellenistic Greek at Birmingham University, and well regarded for his studies on John, sets forth in his latest book the point, "The object of faith in the Johannine, as in the Pauline, message is nearly always Jesus." [16] In Him the very nature of God is made visible. Let us now turn to the Synoptic scholar William Manson of the University of Edinburgh, and learn from him of the eternal nature of our religious dependence on Jesus. This scholar has come to believe that no other teaching, were it compared to Christ's, could last very long. For in listening to Him "we are brought face to face with *God,* and what we experience as the critical and momentous new thing is the direct and inexorable quality of the issue put before us—for or against God's will

[16] W. F. Howard, *Christianity According to John,* Philadelphia: The Westminster Press, 1946, p. 158.

to reign." [17] There is a luminous transparence disclosed at this point of history and of our life-history. In Him and through him, *God*. How we understand now the surrender of even the doubting Thomas, as he uttered the moving, "My Lord and my God"!

There *is* light beyond the "vast black veil," uncertain no longer. To this Light our Bible leads us at the very point where "the great Doer of redeeming things" breaks in upon our lives. As our groping comes to a glorious fulfilment in the splendor of that Light, lo and behold, the Light of the world, the Christ! How may we prevent, how would we want to prevent, our hearts from quickening in devoted worship? Turgenev might have been right when he visualized the face of Christ as "a face like all men's face." Yet we realize—and our source is the comment Charles Lamb is imagined to be making in Hazlitt's charming essay *Of Persons One Would Like to Have Known*—that "there is only one other Person; . . . if Shakespeare were to come into the room we would all rise to meet him. But if that Person were to come into it, we should all fall down and try to kiss the hem of His garment."

A TENSION ACKNOWLEDGED

Our aim in the present lecture has been chiefly to guide in some measure, whether by presenting added information or urging action, those among us who had

[17] William Manson, *Jesus the Messiah, op. cit.,* pp. 209, 210.

thus far centered their attention on the Greek focus, but were inclined to regard that other, the Hebrew-Christian focus, more highly than heretofore.

Admittedly there is a tension between the two. They contrast rather sharply in their outlook on the universe, on history, including the individual's life-history, and on the human soul. The religion each sets forth varies fundamentally from the other, and this lecturer has emphasized particularly, and intentionally so, such differences. He was anxious to make his point and thereby to dispel a confusion which, on this subject, is generally widespread. It must not be permitted to reappear in the present consideration if the great issue of salvation raised in the Bible is to be taken seriously, as it surely must.

Charles Kingsley, in his historical novel *Hypatia,* has at one point restored in a most suggestive scene a sermon by Augustine. In the audience is a man, Raphael, a Greek intellectual of Jewish extraction, who as yet is unbelieving. Like many others in Alexandria, he has come to see and hear the famous scholar whose name is on every lip. Having spent some minutes over the inscription of a psalm, Augustine presently allegorizes it. He makes it mean something which it never did mean in the writer's mind, and which undoubtedly it could never mean, for the speaker has founded his interpretation on a mistranslation at the very outset. I now quote from Charles Kingsley: Augustine

"punned on the Latin version, derived the meaning of
Hebrew words from Latin etymologies. As he went on
with the psalm itself, the common sense of David
seemed to evaporate in mysticism." Meanwhile, our unbelieving Greek out there in the audience began to
wonder where was the learning for which Augustine
was so famed? Yet, gradually, Augustine's hints became more practical and pointed. There appeared in
his reasoning a real and organic connection in what
at first had seemed mere arbitrary allegory. Now,
evolving from the psalm, amid such allegories and
overstrained interpretations, there emerged the unheard-of assertion of a Living, Present God. By now,
our Greek brother really was puzzled, but he reddened
nevertheless with Hebrew pride. "What if Augustine
were right after all? What if the Jehovah of the Old
Scriptures were not merely the national patron of the
children of Abraham, as the rabbis held; not merely,
as Philo held, the Divine Wisdom which inspired a
few elect sages, even among the heathen; but the Lord
of the whole earth and of the nations thereof?" What
if Augustine's hints were to the point? But more. What
if Augustine were right in going even further than
Philo? What if this same Jehovah, Wisdom, Logos,
call him what they might, were actually the God of
the spirits, as well as the bodies, of all flesh? What if
he were near to the heart of men, yearning after souls?
"What if he loved man as man, and not merely one

favored race or one favored class of minds? And in the light of that hypothesis, that strange story of the Cross of Calvary seemed not so impossible after all." [18]

Yes, what *if* . . . ? Could it be that these questions are *our* questions? Is it at all possible that what we have come to see now from the new Hebrew-Christian outlook has direct reference to the things that really matter to us—those things which we had felt were heretofore left out of the picture?

Yes, what *if* . . . ?

[18] Charles Kingsley, *Hypatia*, New York: A. L. Burt Company, pp. 307, 311.

CHAPTER VI

The Path Across This Wilderness

If the Bible Pattern Were True . . .

I always enjoy Aristotle's suggestion that virtue rather than honor is the end of political life, and also his admission that such virtue seems actually compatible with being asleep or with lifelong inactivity.[1] But, then, Aristotle adds, a man leading such a life could not be called happy unless he were maintaining a thesis at all costs.[2] In Aristotle's consideration, happiness is identified with virtuous activity. He points out that "in the Olympic Games it is not the most beautiful and the strongest that are crowned, but those who compete."[3] Only they who act, win, and rightly so, the noble and good things of this life.

It is noteworthy that the parable of the athlete is also found in the New Testament in the Second Letter to Timothy. "An athlete is not crowned unless he competes according to the rules" (2 Tim. 2:5). This is the whole point, but what are these rules, and where do

[1] *Ethica Nicomachea, op. cit.,* Book I, 5, 1095b.
[2] *Ibid.,* I, 5, 1096a.
[3] *Ibid.,* I, 8, 1099a.

they originate? We read further: "I have fought the good fight, I have finished the race. I have kept the faith. Henceforth there is laid up for me the crown of righteousness, which the Lord, the righteous judge, will award to me on that Day, and not only to me but also to all who have loved his appearing" (2 Tim. 4: 7, 8).

On first notice, the language seems to be very much the same, but the context is different. Having made of his life a work of art, the Aristotelian man will prove a good citizen, and, if qualified, will enter into the active contemplation of the life of the mind. The Christian man realizes that, having made of his life a muddle until the day of his redemption by the Saviour, he has hopes of a richer prize in the new life, and that only then will schemes of earthly improvements begin to take on meaning and reality.

We may discern which of these two is right, only when we discover what is the "light beyond the curtain." Is it the glow of a fixed star, many light-years away and without relevance to our own lives, or the Light of the world breaking through our individual lives in the Person and mighty Works of the Lord? As we have seen before, the issue cannot be avoided. It is "either-or," not "both . . . and."

The issue is made real as we hear that "If it were true, after all," from Charles Kingsley's account breaking in on us like an insistent echo. Yes, if the pattern of the world within the Biblical framework were true, what then? What would be the outcome in your life and mine? This is no rhetorical device for a preacher's dialectics, but the yes-and-no simplicity demanded when vital questions are set forth.

And because the issue is clear-cut, we find it raised in every walk of life; and because it is vital, we find it actually, one way or another, settled in every life. I realize, therefore, that I must dwell on the thought that the inner motives actually at work in my own life are proclaimed by the way I live it. I must "stop, look, and listen." Emerson has somewhere a pungent remark on this, to the effect that what we do speaks so loud that people are unable to hear what we say. Which further proves that we must give our lives more than a second thought.

We may see an indictment of our sophistication and inhibitions in the fact that inner motives seem to be disclosed freely only in children, as it were, and even there only on occasion. That is why the Bible says, A little child shall lead us. A recent illustration of this truth will interest our returned veterans, many of whom now live on the campus with wife and child. It is the real story of a little girl who woke up afraid in the middle of night and cried out for her father. Said the father, taking her in his arms, "Don't be afraid. God is protecting you."

"Yes, Daddy," the child answered with one last sob,

"but when I am afraid, I want *someone with skin on!*"

I know of no better initiation into the mystery of Incarnation. And as this little child has prompted me to candid frankness, I must say that just such a remark as hers might help us to reconciliate the sophomores and the divinity men mentioned in our first lecture. Let the divinity men begin to show on the campus their Lord and His way, *with skin on,* then maybe, some day, some of the sophomores might even become candidates for the ministry, and get around to studying theology. Who can tell?

Because the issue raised by the pattern set forth within the Bible is, after all, a simple issue, we said a while ago that it must of necessity be settled in every walk of life. Let us make good that assertion by quoting the confession of Paul S. Minear, a professor of theology, in a recently published book entitled *Eyes of Faith:*

"I have been increasingly impressed by what could be briefly stated as: (1) the strangeness of the Biblical perspective; (2) the unity of this perspective throughout the Biblical period; (3) the futility of trying to understand any segment of thought detached from its hidden context; (4) the germinal power and universal relevance that emerges whenever that context is uncovered and appropriated; (5) the unsuspected value of the more objectionable patterns of thought in locating distinctive dimensions.

"I may say that each of these convictions has been forced

upon me against my own inclination; when I started the study of the New Testament I had almost the opposite expectations. Over and over again, I have been chagrined to have my convictions reversed. When I have been most certain that I understood Isaiah or Jesus, because a particular teaching seemed to agree with my fund of opinions, I have in fact been farthest from understanding them. Over and over again, confidence that a particular strand in Biblical thought was outmoded has been negated. Gradually I have been taught that any interpretation of an apostle is unsound unless it springs from a personal (and necessarily subjective) comprehension of the apostle's point of standing within his own history. And finally the suspicion dawned that perhaps the strange history within which the apostle stood *is* the true history within which I too stand. This suspicion has prompted so many intimations of the true dimensions of my own existence that I am impelled for my own sake to try to think through the various ramifications of the Biblical perspective." [4]

Yes, if the Biblical perspective were the true perspective,[5] your life and my life would then become totally involved in that perspective, and we should proceed on it. The best imperative will always be an indicative. To be out of the truth is to be in the wrong. Thus we find Paul's life summed up in his words to Agrippa:

[4] Paul S. Minear, *Eyes of Faith*, Philadelphia: The Westminster Press, 1946, p. 2.

[5] In this connection cf. an excellent series of articles by James D. Smart in *The Journal of Religion*, v. 23, 1943, under the title "The Death and Rebirth of Old Testament Theology."

"I was not disobedient to the heavenly vision" (Acts 26:19).

What both deeds and words mean in terms of righteousness is fulfilled in the prominence given by our Lord to the proclamation of the Kingdom of God. On this most impressive feature of the New Testament we now pause.

The Spell of Righteousness

At this point, moreover, a constant element of the Messianic hope runs from the Old to the New Testament, namely, the teaching on the Remnant. The Kingdom of God is revealed in a wealth of parables illustrating its desirability, its infinite worth, its uncompromising requirements, and, by the same token, the great parting of the ways implied therein. The resulting judgment appears to be one which the individual actually pronounces upon himself, according as to whether his way of life henceforward involves the acceptance, or the rejection, of the Kingly Rule which is incarnated in Jesus. Let it be known that the word "orthodoxy" refers to life, first the real inner life, beginning at home with the individual. "Not everyone who says to me, Lord, Lord, shall enter the kingdom of heaven, but he who does the will of my Father who is in heaven. On that day many will say to me, Lord, Lord, did we not prophesy in your name, and cast out demons in your name, and do many mighty works in your name? And then will I declare to them, I never knew you: depart from me, you evil doers!" (Matt. 7: 21-23) By the way, that is hardly the way a far-off mystic would speak. Those who seek refuge in the Sermon on the Mount so as to steer away from a Divine Jesus choose the worst possible course. Who is He who represents Himself as sitting in judgment on all the earth in the last day? Surely not just a kindly mystic who does his best to "hit upon" right notions as to what the Kingdom might be comparable! Professor Henry J. Cadbury is right when he warns us against "the peril of modernizing Jesus"!

As the Good Shepherd gathers in His flock, we are reminded that in the East the word "shepherd" was commonly used to describe the bringer of salvation. The Messianic King who is "the way, the truth, and the life" is all three at the same time. He is identified with salvation. Christianity is summed up in His name. Through Jesus, the Kingdom of God, in Otto's excellent reconstruction and translation of Matthew 11: 12 and Luke 16: 16, "exercises its force." *He* is the Kingdom, because our redemptive God is even now at work in and through Him. The Kingdom of God, then, is the mighty Power of Him whose workshop is human history and, therefore, our own life-history; of Him whose will should be done on earth as it is done in heaven. It is, at the same time, above, within, and beyond history. *Within* history, that is, so far as we are directly concerned for the present, our Lord's Kingly Rule is at work among us. It is then our business to play our part in this redemptive drama, if we would abide forever. And this is righteousness.

Righteousness implies a new direction in life, that is, a "conversion." The conversion presented in the New Testament is, on the part of God, a new creation, and implies on our part a new birth. There are, as a matter of fact, two ways of looking at the same reality, which is freely offered to us in Christ. Having secured a solid foothold in this reality, the new man is filled with the most genuine joy. Nay, his assurance of "doing the truth" gives him a foretaste of eternal life. He learns that, just as he once was dead in the midst of life, he may some day be alive in the midst of death. Already, as he approaches the narrows, a Helping Hand has clasped the outreaching of his whole being, and is drawing him on till he becomes truly a "man of the other side." Behold, the taste of milk and honey from beyond this wilderness sweetens his breath. He now lives in a new dimension of life, which makes him, even now, partake of eternal bliss.

A FAITH ACCESSIBLE TO STUDENTS

This faith is directly accessible to the liberal arts student who understands that he cannot live by "brains" alone, and is willing to be made whole again. The tran-

sition is far from being a painful one. To walk under
the Kingly Rule we need only take the easy yoke. To
the Carpenter of Galilee, who knew how to make
them, a yoke was not "a badge of servitude, but a con-
venience, a method of carrying the burden in an easier
manner, so that the burden seems light." [6] This last
analogy we borrow from William Lyon Phelps, who
heard of it from Henry Drummond as the latter, speaking at Yale in the autumn of 1887, made the deepest
impression on the students Phelps had ever noted.
What the Yale students heard had to do with "a little
group of young missionaries who went into a far
country and never mentioned religion either in
speeches or in conversation. They engaged in business
and tried to live like the Master. After a year of this,
the natives kept coming to their house to find out the
guiding principle of their lives, what they believed
that made their daily conduct different from others and
kept them so cheerful." Drummond was persuasive, his
position being that we do not need advocates for
Christianity so much as we need *witnesses*.[7]

The story told by Drummond to the students at Yale
is a common illustration of a basic feature in the Christian life. And as Drummond came from Scotland, we
might set beside his example that of an elderly lady
who asked for membership in a church in Dundee.

---

[6] William Lyon Phelps, *Autobiography with Letters*, op. cit., p. 200.
[7] *Ibid.*, p. 202.

When questioned regarding her conversion, she replied that she had heard Dr. McCheyne, the eminent Scotch preacher, exclaim, as he prayed, "O Lord, Thou knowest that we love Thee," and that she could see by his shining face that he meant it.

Why, students themselves are familiar with such an experience. In a group of West Point delegates at Northfield someone raised the question, "What is Christianity?" There was silence for a while, and then one student replied, "Oscar Westwood." You see, Oscar Westwood was the sort of witness Henry Drummond had in mind, in the story just referred to. Some years ago, a youth named Wray entered Princeton as a volunteer for foreign mission work. Once in the mission field, he simply lived the Christian life before the natives. And one day, according to the custom in that country, some of these natives were seated in a circle on the ground, listening to the instruction of one of their teachers, when the question was brought up, "What is it to be a Christian?" And no one could answer. Finally, a native pointed to where this young worker sat, and replied, "It is to live as Mr. Wray lives." Not one of them could read the Gospel according to Matthew, Mark, Luke, or John, but every one there could read the Gospel "according to Wray." The Bible has it that the truth authenticates itself by taking possession of the individual soul. "Thou follow me."

It has been truly said of the great Dante that he did not possess a faith so much as it possessed him.

It is like this: provided we begin to walk in the right direction, we begin to appropriate the truth, only to realize that we ourselves are being appropriated by the truth. In every realm of endeavor it will be realized that action is a way of learning, inasmuch as it precedes apprehension of learning. We act our knowledge before we actually grasp it. But while this is true of common notions, it is still more so of the higher notions. There is deep significance in Goethe's assertion that the highest cannot be spoken; it can only be acted! The contrary also is true. Suppose the highest loses its true character, then a divine meaning degenerates into mechanical gestures. Nay, sacraments take on aspects of magic as soon as the awareness of their true reference has been lost.

At this point, students should be warned against a wrong interpretation of the theory of feeling and will expounded by the Danish physiologist, Dr. Lange, and by William James, notably in chapter XXIV of his *Principles of Psychology*. It is the theory according to which the outward expression of any emotion leads to the experiencing of that emotion itself, and also to the ideas with which the emotion is associated. It is quite wrong to speak, in this connection, of *autosuggestion* as we speak of the Christian experience. The truth within the paradox lies in the fact that there is authentic ground for that experience. The first steps taken are only meant to open a channel for the Grace of God.

What we are saying here is simply this: provided we walk in the right direction and "do the truth," then the truth comes to us and takes possession of us. John Wesley, referring in his *Journal* to the famous Aldersgate Prayer meeting, declares that he went there "very unwillingly," but he went, thus placing himself in the path of divine mercy. The *Journal* continues by recalling that someone at the meeting read Luther's preface to Paul's letter to the Romans. "About a quarter of nine, while he was describing the change which God works in the heart through faith in Christ, I felt my heart strangely warmed. I felt I did trust in Christ, Christ alone, for salvation; and an assurance was given me that *He* had taken away *my* sins, even *mine,* and saved *me* from the law of sin and death." This testimony appears all the more valuable when you remember that by temperament John Wesley was a sceptic. It was said of him, moreover, that he never was carried away by the emotions he aroused in others. "The Holy Club" which he had formed was not by any manner of means a club of mystics but one of realists. The members read the Greek Testament and the classics, and fasted on Wednesday and Friday. Every week they partook of the Lord's Supper and brought all of their life out in the open to be viewed in the light of Scripture.

A committed life, such as John Wesley's, is led along the path of Biblical categories. That is why it is so fruitful. And, again, that is why it is so important to lead back to such categories the wandering mystics, so that they might be reoriented and their quest might prove more to the point. For does the main line of so forceful an experience as John Wesley's lead merely to mystical enjoyment? Emphatically *no*. It leads straight to the open road. For more than thirty years Wesley traveled, altogether, over a million miles, mostly on horseback. He crossed the Irish Channel forty times, wrote more than two hundred books, and preached something like forty thousand sermons.

And what was the gist of his preaching? We may surmise that which was particularly close to his heart by witnessing one of the most moving scenes in the history of the Church as Wesley preached from the village churchyard, standing on his father's tombstone. And here was his subject on that memorable occasion: "The kingdom of heaven is not meat and drink; but *righteousness,* and peace, and joy in the Holy Ghost."

Neither was righteousness, to him, a means to that end—peace and joy. Such blessings were merely added to it. In direct contrast to the mystic, who would loose the shackles of his own humanity, the Bible Christian realizes that great human crusades for deliverance from evil find their meaning in that foretaste of eternal life which here is expressed in righteousness. On Wednesday, February 23, 1791, Wesley wrote his last letter, addressed to Wilberforce and urging the latter to carry on his crusade against the slave trade.

We may here glean sufficient inspiration to enable us to map our way out of the wilderness of this life.

ALONG THE FENCED-IN PATH

The new pilgrim needs must shun the road to the village named Morality. He will enter, rather, through the straight and narrow path "cast up by the Patriarchs, Prophets, Christ, and His Apostles"; and there will be stretching forth before him a way "as straight as a rule can make it."

We can see right by the Wicket Gate, Good-will directing him to the House of the Interpreter. In the person of the Interpreter the Christian student may recognize the greatest philosopher of the ancient world and of all times—the best known, historically speaking, of all the great men of antiquity, except, perhaps, Cicero—I mean Paul, the Apostle. On leaving the House of the Interpreter, the Christian student will be enlightened as never before, and realize fully that he is running in opposition to the ways of the world. This will not make his progress easy at first, but, then, he is not an appeaser—he is a pilgrim.

The highroad, up which we must go, is "fenced on

either side with a Wall, and that Wall is called Salvation."

So it is a changed pilgrim who plods upward to the Cross, at the very foot of which his burden will fall from his shoulders. "Here beginneth a new life"—his sins forgiven, stripped of his Rags, *cloathed* with Change of Raiment, a mark on his forehead, and, in his hands, a Roll with a seal on it—which later he will present at the Celestial Gate. No longer is it his ambition to do as everyone else does. He has denied, nay, literally, disowned, himself. Henceforward, for him "to live, is Christ."

The pilgrim knows in whom he has believed, and so what the world calls death for him has lost its sting. Let us remember that *Scio cui credidi* became Pascal's motto. From within the boundaries of the Delectable Country, death now appears as a dawn which widens and brightens an uninterrupted vision.

The Christian student, as such, to all practical purposes will shy away from all forms of syncretism that beckon him from either side of the Wall of Salvation. For he is determined to continue in the primitive and most authentic tradition that has generated and sustained to this very day the expansion of Christianity, *i.e.,* the message of the finality of Jesus Christ. He recalls that the doctrinal pronouncements of the Early Church, and through the ages down to those of the Westminster divines, were meant to be so many buttresses in the fence that guards the Way against the encroachments of Hellenism. Nevertheless, he will make a point of learning the philosophic grammar and methods of the Greeks in order to continue protecting the Way still more adequately. A good, up-to-date, streamlined fence might appear to be unfamiliar, but, as a matter of fact, it will be the same.

SHUNNING MOURNFUL NOTIONS

As we now see the Christian student he may perhaps be justifiably weary of the mournful representations of his Saviour by countless artists ever since medieval times. It is noteworthy that, as the primitives of the Middle Ages strove to bring out an agonizing inner conflict and mortal sadness in the Divine Face, their dramatic sense paved the way for the affectation of the Italian Renaissance as well as for the morbid excesses of the Spanish school. There are so many ways of losing Christ! It must, indeed, be emphasized that a growing awareness of the sufferings on the Cross had intensified throughout the Middle Ages feelings of reverence for the Broken Body. It must also be acknowledged that such an awareness found a unique expression in the spiritual quality of Christian art in the fifteenth century, as it brought out the grievous and heartbreaking character of the Redeemer's sacrifice. While this was done with depth and perfect restraint, it nevertheless singled out and magnified the tragedy of death and sorrow. The horror reached a point of caricature and despair in the weird realism of German primitives.

Although *Imitation of Christ* should be one of those priceless books we read each passing year, and whence we inevitably gain great blessings for our individual meditation, still a sense of gloom and martyrdom pervades that unique masterpiece of personal religion—the very same emotions that loom forth in such magnificent works of art as *Calvary,* or *Descent from the Cross,* or the *Pietà* by the Master of Avignon. Belief in good works and sacerdotalism appear to be responsible for a tenseness too rarely relieved by the awareness of the Glory of the Gospel message.

The true figure of Jesus Christ has often been dimmed or lost in art because it had been dimmed or lost in theology and in everyday life. Throughout the centuries men have recreated in their own image and likeness "the most beautiful of the sons of men." Such mournful representations of the Christ will doubtless suggest corresponding types of discipleship to the Christian student. "What availeth it to live long, when there is so small amendment in your lives?" sighs the author of *Imitation of Christ.* "Alas! length of days doth more often make our sins the greater, than our lives the better!" The pious monk then proceeds to show the proof of his assertion: "Many there are who count how long it is since their conversion; and yet full slender oftentimes is the fruit of amendment of life." (1, 23). Such despondency will rather be a warning to the Christian student.

A Congenial Atmosphere

At the Christian student's bedside I would like to see, next to the Bible, Bunyan's *Pilgrim's Progress*[8] from which we have already quoted. He will come to recognize in this book the most authentic classic and *vade mecum* of the Reformed faith. In it he will never find one ounce of Greek mysticism or the least compromise of scholasticism. Yet, in its vivid Hebrew imagery, Bunyan's masterpiece will prove to be strangely up-to-date.

Students on either side of the Way may smile at such lack of sophistication and make pronouncements with pebbles in their mouths; but the Christian student will not mind being looked down on as a "fool." One of his good qualities is humility. What he will like most of all in *Pilgrim's Progress* is its congenial atmosphere, a type of environment to which his new organism is adapted.

The Christian student should not only be second to none in the realm of scholarship, but, in ordinary circumstances, he should be well-read. The best that has been written in world literature is not too good for

[8] The Peter Pauper Press, Mount Vernon, New York, has put out an inexpensive attractive edition with illustrations redrawn from the set of woodcuts which appeared in successive early editions about 1700.

him. He will read a great deal of it, and read it to
good purpose.

THE DIET OF A NEW ORGANISM

And so we would further suggest that, although he
will take with many a "grain of salt" all theses that
make the teaching of evolution trespass beyond the
borders of biology—where it originated and where it
belongs—the Christian student might well ponder over
such a book as Bergson's *Creative Evolution*. He might
make his own so precious a piece of information as
this: while elementary forms of life such as the amœba
remain imprisoned in the nutritive environment which
insures their existence, 'advanced' forms of life carry
within themselves the proper means of selecting a
congenial diet. Of course, the student knows that he is
such an 'advanced' form of life. He will now proceed
to learn that Bergson's data on the life of the body
apply still more in reference to the life of the mind and
spirit.

In a healthy mind and spirit, also, there should be
an equilibrium, a state of normalcy. Now, it is noteworthy that a living cell is a closed cell, although, with
the utmost care, it permits certain exchanges essential
to life to take place. So also the human body is protected by the skin, as inner organs are protected by
proper tissues or membranes. Now, whenever a wound
is inflicted, whereby such protection is temporarily

removed, the body runs a fever. In a similar fashion, the mind and spirit which are allowed to be constantly irritated and bruised, and thus exposed against their natural habits, do, in effect, run a fever. And on occasion mysticism might prove to be just such a fever.

The open mind is not a drafty room; neither is it a "dump." There is proper food to be taken in and made our own, according to the type of reborn organism we have. There are poisons to be eliminated. There are wounds to be healed. Above all, there is a healthy mind and spirit to be kept healthy.

An Expectant Mind

The Christian student will learn from those whose life-work has become a tribute to what true Biblical humanism can be.

He will learn from such men as Tertullian, who thought of Christianity as of the highest philosophical wisdom attained by man. He will learn from such giants as Augustine, whose erudition and commitment make him a Christian model worthy of imitation. He will learn from Dante, for whom education was no banquet, but a discipline put to the test in the midst of stirring events. With Thomas Aquinas he will understand that the Christian scholar is a reverent man who safeguards a sense of worship and liturgy as well as the prerogatives of the liberal arts. He will call to mind that so great a reformer as Calvin was at first a fine scholar of the Renaissance. In an age when the common man has been called "the forgotten man," the Christian student will remember John Bunyan as one who was gladly listened to by the people, although despised of the gentry; as one, moreover, who could match wits with learned judges and leave them baffled; then spend twelve years in jail rather than surrender one principle. He will read *Paradise Lost,* and discover a book of universal knowledge comparable in scope to Dante's *Commedia.* John Wesley, with his genius for organization and his full commitment to the service of the Master, will exemplify in the eyes of the Christian student a devoted Christian worker at his best. Gladstone will dazzle him "by the endless versatility of his mind and interests as man of action, scholar, and controversial athlete; as legislator, administrator, leader of the people; as the strongest of his time in the main branches of executive force, strongest in persuasive force; supreme in the exacting details of national finance; master of the parliamentary arts; yet always living in the noble visions of the moral and spiritual idealist." John Morley, from whose pen I borrow this last sketch of Gladstone, makes it clear that such depth and versatility was part and parcel of Gladstone's religious life. It was religion that prompted literary activity and that remained the motive of social duty; and that religion was steeped in Christian tradition from its early centuries. Finally, and above all, he stood firm "in the old Christian faith." [9] But many names follow his, and why pursue an endless enumeration?

The point we have been making here is that, far from belonging to some dark ages of civilization, Christianity is *the* one path that throws light across our dark ages. And the reason is that this narrow path, as "straight as a rule can make it," and "fenced on either side by the Wall of Salvation," finally leads the pilgrims over the Delectable Mountains into the Country where the Sun shineth night and day.

[9] John Morley, *The Life of William Ewart Gladstone* in 3 v., v. I, ch. 6, 184, 204.

CHAPTER VII

"Doing the Truth"

WHAT SHALL WE DO WITH THE TRUTH?

SHOULD THE PRESENT SERIES of lectures end at this point, they could be said to have presented but a caricature of Christianity. The Christian faith is not a subject to talk about; it is a reality upon which we must proceed. The supreme test of these lectures will be found in their outcome. Here ends the spoken word; here ends the book; but only "he who does the truth comes to the light" (John, 3, 21). The old invitation still stands; the divine process of salvation whereby the Call of the Gentiles proceeds, remains the same. Greeks as well as Jews are being gathered in from the highways and byways, that the Lord's House might be filled. They enter on the inheritance of Israel, they are gathered in as they come to the Light. Now this process of coming to the Light is identified with that of "doing the truth."

We would emphasize at this point the strangeness of this pungent Hebrew phrase, "doing the truth." For all practical purposes we usually isolate the terms "doing" and "truth." What do we like to do with truth, for instance? As already stated, we often ignore it while paying it lip service, or we play with it. At a higher level in the life of the mind we earnestly apply ourselves to finding it; having found it, we glory in it; we are proud to be called learned. Reaching to the realm of practice, we devise schemes of applied science or of social reform, that is, we advocate the practice of truth by others. Do we ever reach the point where knowing and doing become one and the same thing in our life and practice, nay, in our being? Again, when we speak of knowing, what object do we name as a complement to the verb? We often do what everybody else does. Such dread of innovation we share in common with "primitive" societies. Impressed with a moral concern, we may try to typify the gentleman admired in our social group and become truly "moral." Such moral qualities we may even take as ends in themselves, so as to make, in true Aristotelian style, a work of art out of our life. The reading of Micah may initiate us into true righteousness; yet further attempts at such righteousness are likely to persuade us that without the Lord we can do nothing. In Him, and in Him only, do we find the doing and the knowing identified. Answering at this point a question raised by students in our first lecture, we may now say not only that Christianity matters, but that in Christianity our whole being is at stake.

Some of you may wonder at this point why it is that

we have come so far toward the end of this series without referring to the great issues of our day. Since the Christian is essentially a committed man, why is it, you may ask, that this lecturer has not raised his voice on the problem of race discrimination, on the exploitation of labor, or on the control of atomic energy? My answer is that if we seek first the Kingdom of God and His righteousness, all such concerns "shall be added" unto us. The word of commission is inseparable from the word of truth. Moreover, it is always an *individual* word of commission. When William B. Booth surrendered to His Lord the Salvation Army was born. The great danger is precisely in stressing action, our own views about action, before the heart and mind have been set right.

G. Campbell Morgan has a great page on the subject in his book *The Crises of the Christ.* In the law of God, according to him, the order is always: worship, trust, bread. That order was inverted by the devil, as shown in the temptation of our Lord. We should, therefore, enter the path of service in the fulness of the Spirit. Thus in resolute abandonment to, and abiding in, the Will of God, consciousness of power will be the inevitable consequence. Let us well mark the proper order, then, because therein lies hidden the secret of a true Christian life. Fulness of the Spirit *becomes* the power of the Spirit, which is to say that fulness of the Spirit must come first if we would "do the truth." Thus the keynote of the Synoptic Gospels is the Kingdom of God, the Kingly Rule, the easy yoke; that of the Fourth Gospel is "life everlasting"; and that of Paul, to be in Christ.

And these are, basically, one and the same thing.

"For to Me to Live is Christ"

Paul's Letter to the Philippians was written from prison by a committed Christian to committed Christians. The text I have chosen to leave with you as a motto at the close of these lectures is, in fact, the key-verse of that Epistle: "For to me to live is Christ" (1: 21). The second part of the verse, "and to die is gain," merely brings out in bolder relief the full impact of the statement that immediately precedes. Life having once been identified with the Christ, not only does death lose its sting, but it appears in its true light as the dawn which widens and heightens an uninterrupted vision. The phrase, "And to die is gain" is then seen to be a corollary of the proposition, "For to me to live is Christ."

To live and to live right, to take your own place in the stream of life which carries you and surrounds you, surely this is your ambition at this time. "Here beginneth a new life." I need not and will not worry lest any of you should take a cynical approach to your future. For surely none of you is likely to laugh off what has been said in these lectures with the statement, alas too often heard in the world outside, "Anyhow, I want to live my own life," implying a selfish attitude and one assuredly foreign to your individual preoccupations.

So far you have had the opportunity of an education second to none, and you are young. You are now at the age which one may call the "generous" age. Apart from what some of you may have seen in Europe or in the Pacific, no sordid experience of human vicissitude and misery has as yet spoiled your outlook. Let me warn you here and now, however, that unredeemed human nature being what it is, you will know, at one time or another, the pangs of discouragement, the anxieties and hopelessness which sweep over you when everything you hold dear seems then to be doomed to failure. Ah! that is a terrible experience, but it is sure to come to you. I would, therefore, prepare you for it as I take leave of you. And when you come to your Gethsemane, or rather when your Gethsemane comes to you, as it surely will, may you remember the message a friend was led to deliver to you at this time.

You are still within the boundaries of a blessed land, of a dear country. This committed college will not let you go without sharing with you its challenging vision. This is the gateway to a dear country, and you are enjoying its sense of security. The same note of calm is to be found in the letter Paul wrote to all the saints in Christ Jesus that were at Philippi. As the

Apostle was about to launch into his account of the progress of the Gospel in Rome, of his position, feelings and anticipations, he expressed his thankfulness and joy, his affection and prayers, above all, his supreme assurance. Whatever circumstances were to befall him thereafter, this very essential assurance would be kept in the foreground and remain solid as the rock, sound, and his very own: "For to me to live is Christ."

Given the principle, the rest follows. The first truth is the measure of all the truths that follow. It is also the rule of practice. To know the beginning is to know the end—what we commonly call "the meaning of it all." For we realize in this college that there is a "meaning to it all." We rest assured that life on this planet in general, and our own life in particular, is not "a tale told by an idiot," but that it has a definite Biblical meaning and purpose.

Having passed from death to life, the Christian student himself has a blessed sense of regeneration making him capable of keeping God's commandments. A sense of power over self, of victory over the world, and of inexhaustible love for his brethren is being added to this newly experienced delight in the doing of God's will. Above all, there is the blessed knowledge of having been received into the Father's family, for only in the Son does God become the Father. Let no unscriptural tenet of universalism blind us to the fact that "to all who received him, who believed in his

name, he gave power to *become* children of God."
Now, the Spirit bears witness with the newly redeemed
that he has become and is actually a child of God.
What a glorious experience it all is! With Blaise Pascal
the new man in Christ sighs in a tremendous exaltation of his whole being: "Joy, joy, joy, tears of joy!"

Yet Even a Christian Has Problems

After a time, however, victories are likely to become
fewer and more fleeting. Defeats may come in quick
succession and prove more and more disastrous. It may
then appear that spiritual power is slowly "leaking"
away, although at first this backsliding was secret,
almost unknown to the soul itself. James Caughey tells
the story of how he once lost his power at the tea-table.
There had been nothing harmful in the conversation,
to be sure. Yet as he went away his soul was like a
loosely strung bow. And, as the evening advanced, he
discovered to his great dismay that his efforts were
proving of no avail. Similarly, Samuel L. Brengle, that
holy man of the Salvation Army—and what a beautiful
organization the Salvation Army is!—knew of an
officer who had lost his power during a three-mile
drive to the hall. Again, nothing wrong or trifling had
been said. His comrades had just been talking lightly
of things that had no bearing on the coming meeting,
and when he arrived at the hall he was as dry as an old
bone. Indeed, he prayed a good prayer, but there was

no power in it. All around the atmosphere was one of indifference and emptiness. The Bible reading and the talk that followed were excellent in themselves, but everybody looked listless, careless, and sleepy.

Our "innocent" jokes often have had the same effect. The temptation may then come to try to make up for our experienced lack of spiritual power by a recourse to cleverness, to efforts at eloquence, even to the point of being theatrical and of playing on our audience as an artist would play on his instrument. All the time, however, the feeling and inner conviction will persist, that we are erring, going astray, missing the mark, that, somehow, we have become blind leaders of the blind. A false pride may then lead us to revolt and evil temper. Worldly companions helping, entire backsliding is likely to follow on the backsliding of the heart. And yet all along the Spirit of God will be keeping on striving with our spirit, the result being uneasiness and a deeply-rooted fear, as at the same time we become aware of our loss of influence. We then will begin to realize that we have become divided against ourselves. We are likely to worry. In the Greek New Testament, μέριμνα, care, anxiety, solicitude, implies in fact that which is dividing the mind—μερίζειν τὸν νοῦν.

When Paul exhorts us not to be worried about anything, he means to say that we should not be divided against ourselves. When we worry we magnify our trouble and minimize God's power. In the words of George Müller, "The beginning of anxiety is the end of faith, and the beginning of true faith is the end of anxiety." In other terms, the Christian experience is founded on a rock for whosoever heareth "these sayings" of Jesus and "doeth them." May we not, however, secure a deeper insight into such perseverance? Indeed, God is faithful, and on His side our difficulty is fully met. But it is from our human side that we should welcome a clarification of that divinely ordered process. How are we to regard it from our own point of view?

The Essence of the Experience

One word, which we have heard before many times, will suffice to answer this query, and that is *love*. We have used and abused this word until it seems to have lost a great deal of its meaning. Like every word in the Bible, however, it must be read in the Light of the Spirit if we are to see it where it belongs, namely, in the very center of Christian experience.

Let us read it in the context of the thirteenth chapter of The First Letter of Paul to the Corinthians. If I have not love, "I am a noisy gong or a clanging cymbal. . . . I am nothing. . . . I gain nothing." Strong language, that. "So faith, hope, love abide, these three; but the greatest of these is love." Not love as most people understand it, although, however degraded, the notion always bears testimony to its divine origin, but love as a truly supersensual element. Above the order of matter, Blaise Pascal conceived of the order of mind; but, then, from all matter and minds, according to him, one could not draw forth a feeling of true love: "That is impossible, and of another order, supernatural," he concluded. Love, then, is to be found in the realm of things divine. We know that God is love.

It is on this highest of all planes, on the plane of the uncreated, that we must look for our power to *abide* in the will of God. We are at once impressed by the fact that this creative power which we are now invited to claim, is the very Power that brought everything into existence in such a way that *God saw that it was good*. Again, it is this same Power through which Christ rose from the dead, the first fruits of the Age to Come. Through the same Power we are raised with Him in newness of life. "He who believes in the Son *has* eternal life." In the last analysis, the very essence of the Christian experience is the new life in Christ, this new life being essentially a life of love divine. "For to me, to live is Christ."

Here is the guarantee of our perseverance. To follow our own spiritual growth, therefore, is to witness the stages by which Christ progressively frees us, fighting in us, for us, and through us in the midst of trial and temptation until we reach full stature.

Do you want to discover the secret of St. Patrick's greatness? Read the famous hymn wherein Christ is set in a high sphere as the inspiration of a truly holy man's life and thought:

> "Christ, as a light,
> Illumine and guide me!
> Christ, as a shield, o'ershadow and cover me!
> Christ be under me! Christ be over me!
>> Christ be beside me,
>> On left hand and right!
> Christ be before me, behind me, about me!
> Christ this day be within me and without me!"

This is Christian love; the God-created *agape* which breaks forth in a human life, meeting it in the Christ; not *eros,* not the Greek man-centered mystic quest likely to lose itself in nature after it has proceeded from human nature. The difference between the two, in which culminates the contrast between the Hebrew-Christian approach and the Greek one, has been made the object of Professor Anders Nygren's three illuminating volumes on *Agape and Eros, A Study of the Christian Idea of Love,* published between 1932 and 1939. The work of this Swede deserves careful study and mediation. Those three volumes show that mastery over self can only mean surrender of self to the Master. Until that is done, man stumbles over himself and therefore over Scripture, since the Spirit, which alone gives meaning to the written code, can do so only when self has surrendered itself once and for all.

There, again, we discern what must be the key to our shortcomings as we attempt the highest things. When Leonardo da Vinci painted his great canvas, now known as *The Last Supper,* it happened that he became quite angry with a certain man, whereupon threats of vengeance followed bitter words of resentment, so that the artist could scarcely regain his composure as he again faced his canvas. Yet the most delicate part of his work was now awaiting the touch of genius. He had begun to paint the face of Jesus. There the artist stood powerless, until he understood that, before giving to the Master's face its divine expression, he must first seek out the man whom he had insulted and threatened, and ask his forgiveness. This he did, and then, but then only, was Da Vinci enabled to proceed with the masterpiece.

What is true of the life of the artist is also true of the life of the thinker. Dante affirms that only as Love imparted new power to his mind was the *Commedia* born. In highest love that work was born, and in highest love it grew, ascending at last into the loftiest regions of *Paradiso.* Up there, power could not utter his high fantasy; but already Dante's "desire and will were rolled—even as a wheel that moveth equally—by the Love that moves the sun and the other stars." [1]

---

[1] *The Divine Comedy of Dante Alighieri,* The Carlyle-Wicksteed Translation. Introduction by C. H. Grandgent. Illustrated by George Grosz, New York: The Modern Library, 1932, Random House, 1944, p. 606.

These, as you readily remember, are the closing lines of the last canto.

So universal is Christian humanism that it speaks with equal ease through the common man and through the loftiest aristocracy of the mind; nay, the aristocrat learns from the common man. Read Tolstoy's autobiographical sketch, *My Confession*. See the man renounce the life of his own class because he finds it unreal, because its luxurious superfluity renders comprehension of life impossible. Christian love has made him realize that the simple men around him, the working classes, were the real Russian people. To Count Tolstoy, they make clear at last the meaning of life. Such meaning is so clear, in fact, that it can now be put in the plainest language. And that language is a language of self-surrender in love: "Each of us is so created by God that he may ruin or save his soul. To save his soul, a man must live after God's word by humility, love, and endurance." Such is Tolstoy's testament, for your guidance and mine.

Because it is divine, this creed of love is universal. It is the one creed that really works. Bishop Thoburn once had been a fighter like so many theologians. When as a lad of twenty-one he arrived in India, he hastened to learn the language so as to be able to meet any of the natives in argument. In the long run, however, he came to realize his failure so far as the Christian ministry was concerned. He became, in fact, very unhappy about his mission. So he went in prayer one day and Christ came to him, and said to him in words so real they seemed to have been uttered for him alone, "Go preach my Gospel." From that day young Thoburn quit controversy. He later became one of the most famous missionaries India has ever known. In a speech made in 1901 he summed up his missionary life in this one sentence: "Then it became more and more impressed upon me, as I got nearer and nearer to Christ, that I had never received a mission from Him to argue with anybody; and I remembered my commission, received when I was a boy of twenty-one." [2]

Could it be, then, that this law of Love in which the whole Bible culminates as it culminates with Christ, gives us the key to the understanding of our universe? Do not call this hint sheer emotionalism. I myself have been warning you all along against such mystical emotionalism. Robert E. Speer, whose book on *The Finality of Jesus Christ* I have been recommending to you, introduces us to another modern saint who was for more than a generation Professor of Obstetrics and Gynecology at the Medical School of the University of Edinburgh. Let us listen to the Professor as he presents the medical graduates for their degrees and proceeds with his farewell address to the university, bearing witness to his Christian faith and

[2] Quoted by Robert E. Speer, *The Finality of Jesus Christ, op. cit.,* p. 298.

experience—to him as real as anything he ever attained with lancet or with microscope. Here are his opening words:

"I do not know in what mood of pessimism I might have stood before you today had it not been that ere the dew of youth had dried off me I made friends with the Sinless Son of Man, who is the well-head of the stream that vitalizes all advancing civilization, and who claims to be the First and the Last, and the Living One, who was dead and is alive for evermore, and has the keys of Death and the Unseen. My experience compels me to own that claim. For to me, as to the Reformers who founded this University, and to a countless throng throughout the centuries of all sorts and conditions of men, He has established a vivid and vivifying correspondence with our supersensual environment. He has made us 'see' that at the heart of all things there is a Father's heart." [3]

Here we have a scientist's assertion of what has just been called the law of love, namely that there is a Father's heart at the heart of all things.

Such an assertion makes us understand why life in the Christ is the only life. In it and through it we reach to the heart of all things. And this we can do only in a supreme way when our life is identified with the One who is Love.

After we have been enabled to confess that "to me to live is Christ," however, further discovery of Christian

[3] *Op. cit.,* p. 213.

truth, as well as further progress in the Christian life, will be conditioned by that attitude which John A. Mackay has characterized as quite incompatible with a purely theoretical mode of existence. Our commitment as Christians is most essential to a task well done and to a life well lived. Let us never be ashamed of showing our flag; let us pour a personal meaning into the words of the old hymn "Onward, Christian Soldiers." Nay, let our entire commitment proclaim radiantly that "to me to live is Christ," that is to say, "no longer I; Christ liveth in me." Let our surrender therefore be the most unconditional surrender that ever was, and the cock crow that Peter heard need never be heard in our backyard!

This, then, is the way to a victorious Christian experience which knows of no long face or tired look. There is fire in it from beginning to end—from the time when the Fire on high descends to consume our love offering, until the time when that same Fire is seen burning in the radiant look that shines forth from a surrendered heart.

A NORMAL LIFE

We do not mean to imply that the disciple's life is supposed to be a life of frenzy lived as in a trance. It is a simple life, a normal life, an everyday life.

Indeed, there are great heights in it, moments of exultation, when it pleases the Beloved to favor His own with words of great sweetness surpassing all the knowledge of this world's philosophers and wise men. "Lord God, the holy lover of my soul, when Thou shalt come into my heart, all that is within me will rejoice," exclaims the author of *Imitation of Christ*. True mystics, truly Christian mystics, have known beatitude when after a moment of illumination they have found themselves to be at one with God. To the faithful such intoxication is evidence of the immediateness of the Living God. It leaves no room for doubt in the fortunate human being who now has reached the very heart of the Biblical experience which is also the Center of the Universe. Thus Evelyn Underhill has defined the true mystic as one who participates "here and now in real and eternal life, in the fullest, deepest sense which is possible to man." [4] Yet even a Saint Theresa warns us against supposing that what she calls "spiritual marriage" leads only to present enjoyment. To her, the Christian's communion with God can be enjoyment only "at times." In every-day life it means sharing the divine strength and applying it to all that belongs to the service of the Lord, so that her motto was finally to become "Work, work."

We are aware of the fact that in our day the most authentic experience of exultation in divine love is being more and more psychoanalyzed, and is variously

[4] Evelyn Underhill, *Mysticism*, a Study in the Nature and Development of Man's Spiritual Consciousness, revised edition, New York: E. P. Dutton & Co., 1930, p. 534.

ascribed to abnormal psychology, sociology, and even to the biochemistry of the glands. But this no longer surprises the Christian student. It means simply that here as elsewhere the assertions of the Christian are challenged by naturalism. As we have seen in our second lecture, two outlooks on life are always with us. At first sight, both seem to be equally legitimate in the light of their presuppositions. But we have seen that we must choose between the two, or, to use the famous phrase of Blaise Pascal, "we must wager." To the Christian the "wager" is a matter that has been settled by the intervention of divine grace, while the naturalist remains the one who has eyes to see, but does not see, ears to hear, but does not hear. In this connection the Word of God will always remain the great divider of men. Some will hear it as a message of election, while others will be led by it only to disobedience. Seen in this light, predestination appears first and foremost as the data of experience.

By the same token, no mere theology of experience may be said to provide final proof to the unbeliever. There can be no more a "proof" of the existence of God in this realm than in any other. To any disciple wont to serve God with his mind there can be here as elsewhere only one more category of argument in the impressive testimony already accumulated relating to the existence of God. The fact that God *is* we know from revelation. The Reality of the living God under-

girds the whole Bible proclamation. It is *the* axiom
of all Christian life and scholarship. Like every axiom,
to be sure, it is beyond demonstration. But, then, it is
not an axiom like every other axiom. It is *the* axiom
in a class by itself, and by this we mean that it defies
explanation in so far as to explain is to put it in a class.
The Reality of God is the Principle of all creation.
"In the beginning, God."

The arguments drawn from the fact of the Christian
experience prove especially precious to Christians themselves. Indeed, the experience of nineteen centuries of
Christian life should carry weight with them as they
take their place in this Heavenly Fellowship. What,
otherwise, would be their justification for ever giving
out their own testimony? Especially should they beware of ever being found guilty of waiting anxiously
for the latest reports of the philosophers and scholars
on their Lord's earthly life before even finding out
who He is.

Of the *reality* of the new life in Christ there cannot
be the slightest doubt for one who has ever "tasted
that the Lord is gracious." At a time when he was still
in a state of "utter abandonment from God's side,"
Blaise Pascal distinguished clearly between the move-
ments of divine grace, which he had once known
through an immediate personal experience, and his
own efforts, which proved to be the result of stirrings
within his own mind and reason. "My son," exhorts

the author of *Imitation of Christ,* "mark diligently the motions of Nature and of Grace; for in a very contrary and subtle manner these are moved, and can hardly be distinguished but by him that is spirtually and inwardly enlightened."

With these words begins one of the greatest chapters of *Imitation of Christ.*[5]

GUIDANCE

Being for the most part a simple life, a normal everyday life, the life of the Christian student should not be considered, as it usually is, in its most spectacular aspects. That is doubtless the meaning attached to Hebrews 11: 1: "Now faith is the substance of things hoped for, the conviction of things not seen." Neither need most of us dramatize in Barthian terms the resulting situation of the pilgrim as of one journeying on a dizzying mountain divide, on the border line of two worlds—our world too often perceived as bereft of God, the other world not to be reached save by a blind act of faith. Such a view seems to ignore on the one side the "addressability" of man; on the other, the partial "accountableness" of the God of Jesus Christ. We are known of our God. We see divine realities "in a mirror dimly," but we see. Our lot is to journey up and down, mostly through foggy weather, now encouraged by patches of white, sometimes small and dim, again

[5] Third Book, ch. 54.

growing larger and brighter, at least enough so as to sustain us in the conviction that far up above there is light streaming through a glory of luminous blue, even if at times we happen to become submerged in a dark and threatening cloud. For we know in whom we have believed.

We know it through feeling, to be sure. Yet mere feeling implies at best an intermittent and oftentimes misleading guidance, as it surely does for many a far-off mystic who ignores the Bible revelation. The "guidance" of which such mystics speak often proves to be the fact of their own impulses. The burden of proof is overwhelming at this point and has made the object of our consideration clear throughout these lectures. However, we might dwell thereon a little longer. For example, so sanctified a man as George Müller was impressed by the fact that nine-tenths of our trouble in matters of mistaken guidance was due to the fact that people did not see the need, at the very outset, to get their heart into such a state that it might have no will of its own in regard to a certain matter.

We have been tireless in our insistence that there is great danger of seeking the will of God through impression or "intuitions" blindly ascribed to the Spirit. Let us again read what George Müller has to say on the subject: "If I look to the Spirit alone without the Word, I lay myself open to great delusions also. If the Holy Ghost guides us at all, He will do it according to the Scriptures and never contrary to them." Having been emptied of self, therefore, we should not depend on our varying moods, but seek the will of the Spirit of God through, or in connection with, the Word of God.

THE SOVEREIGNTY OF GOD

Right at the end of *Pilgrim's Progress,* Bunyan discloses that the last thing he saw in his Dream was "that there was a way to Hell even from the Gates of Heaven, as well as from the City of Destruction." This we may now look on as a warning and as a reminder. A warning against any over-optimism through which self might be reasserted, and a reminder of the fact that we cannot defeat God's Purpose.

Now, who was the man pictured in Bunyan's vivid imagery as disappearing in the way to Hell, which opened out in the side of the Hill right at the Gates of Heaven? That man's name was Ignorance. He had devised his own "religious" schemes. In vain had Christian and Hope tried to make him understand the Gospel message and to proceed on it. No, he had his own ideas. The fact is, he was himself greatly shocked at the "intolerance" of the two pilgrims, who were merely trying to help him. Was he not, after all, on the same road with them? They might even, if it suited them, throw themselves into the water at the end of their journey in order to reach the City in the appointed Way; he would follow his own devices right to the end, and then hire the services of a certain Ferry-man called Vain-hope to get him across safely. But that was the last encouragement Ignorance ever received from men; for he was now on the other side. In vain did he fumble in his bosom for his Certificate. He found none. He had none.

In the course of their lifetime Christian and Hope had been led to wonder in pity over the fate of such men. They had seen an abundance of them in their town, whole families, yea, whole streets, and among pilgrims too. Could it be that they all are left without any notion that theirs is a dangerous state? They may, indeed, fear so at times; surely they must; yet, being naturally ignorant, they do not understand that such fears tend to their good, so that right at the beginning they would be made to go safely in the way of the Pilgrimage. But what do they do? Desperately they seek to stifle their uneasiness. With presumption they continue to flatter themselves in the way of their own hearts. Truly "the Fear of the Lord is the beginning of Wisdom," as Christian concludes.

God has spoken. Then the way is clear. It is straight, as straight as a rule can make it. Ignore it, turn away from it, and devise our own, we certainly may. This, however, would imply the violation of the First Commandment, "Thou shalt have none other gods before me." Yet there are so many such gods—apart from the paraphernalia of mythologies. Pride, love of self, love of money are such gods.

Again, I think of Judas Iscariot, who was one of the disciples, as we know. There is deep meaning in the fact that Dante saw him suffering greatest punishment at the bottom of hell, among the three most treacherous men who, according to the poet, ever lived on earth. Of twenty-four categories of sin, treachery against one's lord and benefactor was reckoned the worst by the author of *Inferno*. How much more so when the betrayal is against the Lord!

However tempted I may be to close this series of lectures on a cheerful note, I must not betray your trust, even though sobering thoughts may invade these last moments with you. Thus we are left to wonder at the startling statement from the pen of a Presbyterian, to the effect that were a certain type of preaching allowed to control the Church, then "Christianity would at last have perished from the earth and the Gospel would have sounded forth for the last time." [6] Far be it from me to belittle the importance of orthodox preaching! My awareness of the solemn duty of proclaiming the Gospel may be read throughout the context of these lectures. Yet the kind of affirmation quoted above would seem to defeat its own purpose. It may not be quite so distressing to hear of those evangelists who are said to have "saved" so many people in one evening.

[6] J. Gresham Machen, *Christianity and Liberalism, op. cit.,* p. 8.

But how, pray, can such statements be made in the very sight of God who actually deported His people to Babylon and finally gave away their inheritance to the Gentiles? We can neither "make" God, nor become substitutes for Him. The simple truth is that we are at best unprofitable servants, and our own ways may prove our undoing. We do not "break" the New Covenant. But we may be broken against it. The danger is not so much in man's environment. It is in man himself. The danger is within me and within you. As for those who through "a certain type of preaching" cause one of the little ones who believe in the Lord to sin, we agree that it would be better for them that a great millstone were fastened about their necks and they were drowned in the depth of the sea (Matthew, 18: 6).

These are sobering thoughts indeed. The 1946 Revised Version of the New Testament, used throughout this series, renders 1 John 4: 17 as follows: "In this is love perfected with us, that we may have confidence for the day of judgment, because as he is so are we in this world." The Greek word herein translated "confidence" originally suggested readiness to do anything, thus, utter frankness in "doing the truth," and thereby free access to God and a resulting fearlessness on the part of the believer. But let us make no mistake about it: the *sine qua non* condition of our status as the Lord's free men is our unreserved acknowledgment of the sovereignty of God. *The Reality and Sovereignty*

*of God remain the primary fact behind and above all
the considerations of these lectures.*

Let us, then, like Ernest Psichari, see our life in terms
of the journey of a centurion set under authority,
having under him soldiers, and saying unto one, "Go,"
and he goes; and to another, "Come," and he comes;
and to his slave, "Do this," and he does it. Such faith
as that of the centurion Jesus had not found, no, not
even in Israel.

The centurion type of Christian has only one concern, namely to do the Lord's will in joy and simplicity
of heart. His life is no longer a miserable sequence of
broken vows and vain resolutions. It no longer knows
perpetual effort and struggle. It is a life of love and
power, because it is a completely surrendered life, and
therefore a life in line with the will of God. As such
it abides forever.

When the twilight of our life turns into the Dawn
which brightens and widens our uninterrupted vision,
may Boswell's simple testimony to the life of Samuel
Johnson be applied to our life also: "Amidst all his
constitutional infirmities, his earnestness to conform
his practice to the precepts of Christianity was unceas-
ing, and . . . he habitually endeavored to refer every
transaction to the will of the Supreme being." [7]

With such a plain purpose in mind, then, may we

[7] James Boswell, *The Life of Samuel Johnson*, The Modern Library,
New York, p. 1162.

simply close our series of lectures with this prayer of Dr. Samuel Johnson:

"O Lord, our Maker and Protector, who hast graciously sent us into this world to work out our own salvation, enable us to drive from us all such unquiet and perplexing thoughts as may mislead or hinder us in the practice of those duties which Thou hast required. When we behold the works of Thy hands, and consider the course of Thy Providence, give us grace always to remember that Thy thoughts are not our thoughts, nor Thy ways our ways. And while it shall please Thee to continue us in this world, where much is to be done, and so little is known, teach us by Thy Holy Spirit to withdraw our mind from unprofitable and dangerous inquiries, from difficulties vainly curious, and doubts impossible to be solved. Let us rejoice in the light which Thou hast imparted. Let us serve Thee, O God, with active zeal and humble confidence, and wait with patient expectation for the time in which the soul which Thou receivest shall be satisfied with knowledge. Grant this, O Lord, for the sake of Jesus Christ our Lord. Amen."

Index